To Love, the sweet kiss of life

MAPPING YOUR Romantic Relationships

Discover Your Love Potential

David Pond

2004
Llewellyn Publications
St. Paul, Minnesota 55164-0383, U.S.A.

First Edition
First Printing, 2004

Book design by Donna Burch
Cover art © Digital Stock and Brand X Pictures
Cover design by Kevin R. Brown
Edited by Andrea Neff

Chart wheels were produced by the Kepler program by permission of Cosmic Patterns Software, Inc. (www.AstroSoftware.com)

Library of Congress Cataloging-in-Publication Data (pending)
ISBN 0-7387-0420-2

Llewellyn Publications
A Division of Llewellyn Worldwide, Ltd.
P.O. Box 64383, Dept. 0-7387-0420-2
St. Paul, MN 55164-0383, U.S.A.
www.llewellyn.com

Printed in the United States of America

Other Books by David Pond

Astrology & Relationships
(Llewellyn Publications, 2001)

Chakras for Beginners
(Llewellyn Publications, 1999)

The Metaphysical Handbook (with Lucy Pond)
(Reflecting Pond Publications, 1984)

Western Seeker, Eastern Paths
(Llewellyn Publications, 2003)

Forthcoming Books by David Pond

Mapping Your Creativity
(Llewellyn Publications, 2006)

Acknowledgments

I would first like to acknowledge my clients who have shared their stories of romance with me over the years. I would especially like to acknowledge my wife, Laura, who has shown me that romance that is grounded in love can continue even in a thirty-year marriage.

I would also like to acknowledge Andrea Neff's fine job of editing and I am especially thankful for the role Stephanie Clement has played in making this book and CD become a reality. Stephanie's undaunted enthusiasm for the project has been a steady source of inspiration from the beginning. She also rolled up her sleeves and did much of the editing required to adapt the book to the format required for the CD. Thank you to the entire production crew at Llewellyn for helping to make the normally stressful task of creating a book an enjoyable experience.

Contents

Part Three: Synastry—The Art of Chart Comparison

Charts

All chart data came from AstroDatabank (www.astrodatabank.com).

Getting Started

We are all different, that is obvious. But how often we feel uncomfortable when faced with our differences with others and feel that if one way is right, the other must be wrong. We're not like this when we go out into nature. We can go for a walk on a trail through the woods and enjoy the diversity of all the different types of plants and trees. We don't pass judgment on whether a tree should be taller or shorter, greener or fuller; we just accept the beauty of the diversity. Were it only that easy with people! If you could be that gracious and accepting of people, in all their diversity, you would be the most peaceful person on earth! But it is not that way for us in our everyday relationships. People push our buttons—nature doesn't; people do.

Relationships push our buttons because we have buttons. We have issues that only get activated in relationships. Using astrology as a tool for exploring your relationships, at a minimum provides a framework for exploring every nook and cranny of your personal relationship portrait, and every nook and cranny of the combined energy of a relationship. Each planet represents a different aspect of your total being, and exploring each planet's make-up in your chart gives you a framework for understanding how it all fits together—the joys and the sorrows.

And truth be known, love does hurt, sometimes. Many people have the attitude of "Love is a risk, you might get hurt!" I wish they had been taught the truth, that love does hurt and so does not risking love; that hurts too—the hurt of loneliness. It is not a risk that you might experience some pain on this planet; it's a guarantee!

We've been disempowered by the modern attitude that one shouldn't feel any type of discomfort. This neuters us. We are stronger than this. The pain of loss, the intensity of passion, jealousy, anger—these are not new emotions. But all of a sudden we find ourselves at a place in history where many people have been led to believe they can't handle emotional pain. Well, we can, we are, and we will. We become disempowered when we believe we shouldn't have to feel any discomfort.

Astrology is a way to regain a connection with your whole truth. It helps you reconnect with your soul heritage: the skills, abilities, talents, shortcomings, and challenges that your soul came here to experience. Simply studying your birth chart will help you know the complexity of who you are, and this will have a beneficial impact on all your relationships. If you know yourself from the inside out, you will be less dependent on other people's opinions of you. Sharing the whole you, the real you, could only be beneficial in relationships.

Throughout this book, you will learn how your personal birth chart can unlock the mysteries of what relationships mean to you. Your birth chart is highly individualistic and will give you information about your specific needs, talents, wants, and challenges concerning relationships. Studying your partner's birth chart gives you these same insights into your partner's needs in relationship and provides a tool for understanding why many of the differences between the two of you are absolutely appropriate.

Part One
Basic Astrology

Astrology is a language. Learning astrology is like learning any foreign language. You already have the ideas, concepts, and experiences of your life within you; you are just learning a new language for what you are already experiencing. To learn a language, you need to know its alphabet, and in astrology, this is made up of the planets, signs, houses, and aspects. Think of yourself as being the director of the play of your life. As the director, you have free will to script your play as you choose, but you need to know the nature of the cast you are working with. The actors and actresses are the planets; the signs are the roles the characters came to play; the houses are the settings for this all to take place in; and the aspects reveal how all of the characters get along with one another.

Planets: The characters; the actors and actresses in the play of your life.

Signs: The scripts and roles the characters are to perform.

House: The settings where the characters play out their roles.

Aspects: How the characters either support, or are in conflict with, each other.

Your birth chart itself is a map to all of these players in your life and how they are best staged to work out their individual roles in a way that doesn't interfere with the needs of other players in the chart. Otherwise, problems erupt. Every chart has its inconsistencies. You can explore one part of your chart that describes you in a certain way, and it feels right. You can then explore another part of your chart that describes part of you that is equally true, yet is in conflict with the first part. This typically manifests as challenges in the outer world with others or situations that are an expression of the conflict within your own chart. This goes on until you script a lifestyle that allows for all of these discrepancies in your own life. Then these outer problems seem to disappear, or at least the impact they make on you diminishes.

The point of using astrology is to help you accept what you have been given to work with, and then to help you find healthy ways to incorporate this into your life. Your birth chart is the map to living in harmony with yourself and the world around you. Let's jump in.

1
The Planets—
The Cast of Characters

We all have all the planets in our birth chart. You are just one person, but you also have the same full cast of characters within you that everyone else does. One person, yes, but various voices within you concerning relationships, emotional issues, career, anger, and even the urge to leave it all behind, to name a few. We all have all of these voices and more. In this presentation, I'm encouraging you to consider each of the planets as the various characters in the play of your life, remembering that you are the director. Your astrological birth chart is a map to all of these characters. By studying each of the planets in your chart, you come to know the natural way that each of these planets expresses itself.

The Sun

The leading actor in your play.

The center of the solar system that animates all of life is the same life-generating force in your chart. The Sun is your connection to the most vital aspect of your being—it is that important. Although not the all and everything, this is the part of you that animates and influences all other parts of you, your basic life essence. The sign your Sun is in describes the role you came to perform to feel this most vital connection to life.

The Moon

The leading actress in your play.

The Moon deals with the emotional side of life; thus the sign of your Moon represents your emotional style—how you express your emotions and how you receive emotional expression from others. The Moon also represents your most natural way of responding to change, how you nurture yourself and others, your comfort zone, and the environment in which you would be most comfortable. The Sun is how you project yourself, and the Moon represents the habits you develop to rest, retreat, and restore yourself.

Mercury

The narrator.

Mercury is the messenger and communicator of the planetary family; it keeps the dialogue moving. The condition of Mercury in your chart shows how you gather information, make it useful, and communicate it to others. Mercury's sign reveals your learning style and what you tend to think about. Your Mercury also shows your natural listening abilities.

Venus

The feminine romantic lead.

Venus is both the patron of the arts and the goddess of love. Venus represents your capacity to appreciate and enjoy beauty, and to bring these refinements into your life. It also represents your capacity to receive love and the qualities you are most attracted to in others. It is the part of you that you would most like to share in your close involvements with others.

For a man who hasn't incorporated his inner feminine, his Venus, along with his Moon, will likely describe what he is looking for in a woman. For a woman, Venus represents her attitude of who she is as a woman, which is highly affected by the influence of the important women in her early life.

Mars

The masculine romantic lead.

Mars is your ability to act on your passions and desires. It is your warrior, the male, aggressive, assertive part of your character that represents how you stand up and defend yourself, initiate action, act on your passions, and express your anger and frustration. Mars combined with Venus represents your sexual magnetic field: what you value and want to receive through Venus, and how you go about getting this with Mars.

For a woman who has not yet incorporated her inner masculine, her Mars, along with her Sun, will represent qualities she is looking for in a man. For a man, Mars represents his attitude of who he is as a man, which is often affected by his early male role models.

Jupiter

The adventurer who always wants to expand the plot.

Jupiter, the largest planet, represents how you reach out to participate in a larger reality. The types of beliefs and philosophy that guide you on your path are shown by Jupiter's sign, which also represents where you seek your rewards and opportunities. The condition of your Jupiter also shows how you express your generosity.

Saturn

The rigid authority figure, stern and unbending.

Saturn represents the nature of the challenges you have to face on the way to becoming a full authority in your life. In the early years of life, Saturn represents authority figures in the world around you telling you how you are supposed to be. Ideally, you ultimately internalize your relationship to authority, and Saturn then represents your self-control, self-restraint, and self-discipline. This is what Saturn demands: self-mastery, that's all! Until you have internalized this relationship to authority, you are subject to the approval and disapproval of others, the police, bosses, etc. Your Saturn placement shows where you have fears concerning authority.

Chiron

The mysterious healer who knows things others don't.

Chiron was discovered in 1979; thus we're still learning about its impact on people's lives. The myth of Chiron is that as a young centaur, he was playing with a poisoned arrow and wounded his thigh. This being a potentially fatal wound, he set upon a course of learning everything he could about healing. From dealing with this wound, his destiny of becoming a teacher of healers unfolded. You will find information about Chiron included in the interpretations in the CD-ROM included with this book.

Uranus

The rebel who always wants to stir things up.

Uranus is the rebel, the revolutionary, or the reformer, but never the conformer. It is the voice of the Awakener, who puts situations in front of you that force you to consider reality in a whole new light. Uranus is the cosmic trickster, unpredictable and unexpected.

Neptune

The glamorous illusionist who is not what she appears to be.

Neptune is the urge to escape the trivial concerns of everyday life; the urge for transcendence. As one of the farthest planets from the Sun, Neptune pulls your attention to distant realms. Its vehicle is imagination, which allows you to consider realities that aren't immediately present, from the highs of creative and spiritual inspiration, to the lows of escapism and illusions.

Pluto

The intimidating power figure who's not above using sinister means to get his way.

Pluto is the farthest planet from the Sun in our current understanding of the solar system, and represents those forces in your life that are furthest away from your conscious understanding of who you are. Pluto gives clues to your subconsciously held motivations that compel you to behave in certain ways without your conscious choice. Obviously, this is not the easiest planet to get a grasp on. For the spiritually inclined, Pluto is where you must surrender to the role that you are to act out in the larger play of life;

your soul purpose and destiny. It also represents the parts of your character that you must purge in order to discover your soul purpose. It can represent buried shadow material that is too gruesome for the psyche to hold in the everyday conscious mind.

South Node

People and experiences from the past.

Your South Node describes the skills and talents you brought with you from your own past lives, and often, the experiences of your early family life. The South Node describes the area of life that is familiar and easy, but offers no growth.

North Node

People offering helpful direction for growth.

The North Node points to the area of life that will provide you with soul growth. But this is not familiar or comfortable, so it takes time to learn to draw from this source of food for the soul. It is not so much about effort and making your North Node work for you; growth comes by allowing experiences in the sign and house of your North Node.

2
The Signs—
The Roles You Came to Play

The signs are the twelve archetypal roles through which the planets express themselves. We all have all the signs represented somewhere in our chart, and they reveal the appropriate roles to follow in the area of the chart where they fall.

The Elements: Fire, Earth, Air, and Water

The elements are of key importance in understanding the signs. The elements are the four main qualities of life experience; the cornerstones of the human experience. They are fire, earth, air, and water. When you divide the twelve signs by the four elements, you get three signs in each element, representing the three stages of development of the particular element.

The Fire Element: Aries, Leo, and Sagittarius

Fire needs fuel, and the first thing that is evident of the fire signs is that they are all active signs; they need activity for the fuel to burn. Fire rises upward, and the fire signs all seek to live a life filled with inspiration, which leads to excitement, energy, drive, and an outgoing nature. Fire is the initiating, creative spark around which life coalesces. Where the fire signs fall in your chart is where you should "fire up" and project yourself fully into the affairs of these houses. Fire is the catalyst, the spark that ignites others into action; thus fire signs are often found in leadership positions.

The Earth Element: Taurus, Virgo, and Capricorn

"Down to earth" is a phrase that aptly describes the temperament of the earth signs, and the keywords reflect this: realistic, sincere, genuine, steadfast, organized, and skillful. These are the attributes of earth; nothing fancy, but something very real. This is the element of the builders and the doers who have the patience and follow-through to bring projects to completion. The earth signs demonstrate competence in dealing with the material world, and where they fall in in your chart is where you are willing to be patient in building the quality of life that you believe in. The earth signs take pride in excellence in all they do, and are competent, capable, and reliable. This task-oriented element indicates where you like to stay busy attending to projects.

The Air Element: Gemini, Libra, and Aquarius

The air element is the realm of the mind, and these signs need ideas for nourishment like others need potatoes and carrots. Thinking, talking, writing, and interacting with others are some of the ways in which we engage the air element. This movement of ideas is what most affirms life itself to the air signs. The hunger to learn and to be in intellectually stimulating circumstances is primary. The air signs are the mental gymnasts that can become bored in a lifestyle with too much routine and not enough mental stimulation. Interaction is the key for the air element. There is a strong need to get out and about and among people in the social realm. Where the air signs are in your chart is where you like to stay informed and keep tabs on what is going on.

The Water Element: Cancer, Scorpio, and Pisces

The water signs introduce the emotional level of life, and thus represent the trickiest level of all because of our culture's ineptness in truly understanding the emotional side of life. With the water signs, it is important to accept the fluid nature of the emotional world, which is tidal like the great oceans: high tide, low tide, in rhythmic measure. We think of our emotions as up and down, or good and bad. If you have a strong emphasis on the water element in your chart, learn how to change "up and down" to "outward and inward." What a difference this can make; there is less judgment implied. Water-sign people need to engage in healthy inward-turning activities and need plenty of quality time alone for this, but this is not what the outside world tends to support. Where the water signs are in your chart is where you need to feel, rather than think, your way through.

3
The Houses—
The Settings Where Your
Characters Play Out Their Roles

The houses are the twelve areas that the chart is divided into, showing the settings, or where in life the activity of the planets is to take place. If you don't have any planets in a particular house, it doesn't mean this area of your life will be empty. For example, the First House rules the body, but if you don't have planets in the First House, you will still have a body! It is best to think of empty houses as "neutral zones." By comparison, houses that hold a concentration of planets compel you to the activity of that house. From a spiritual perspective, it could be said that you don't carry any karma in the empty houses; you are free to make of them what you will. Some of the houses, particularly the Seventh and Eighth Houses, deal more directly with the relationship process and will be explored more thoroughly in that light.

The First House and the Ascendant

The First House (also called your "rising sign") shows how you go out to meet the world in anything you do; thus it is vitally important in that it molds how you approach everything. It is not only your most natural way to present yourself to the world, it is also your best way of doing so. Your Ascendant describes your "attitude of approach" toward all that you do.

The First House rules the body and your self-image. It is your most immediate experience of life, where you are most directly aware of your separate sense of self and that which is closest to your self-identity. You will strongly identify with any planets in your First House.

The Second House

The Second House describes the skills, talents, and abilities you develop to provide for your security. This shows your attitude about your own personal resources, including your money, possessions, and the skills you have for acquiring these needs. This is where you need to develop confidence in your ability to provide for yourself. Although this house is not directly related to relationships, indirectly, the personal security that you experience will have a huge impact on your relationships. To feel security, you must take it out of the future and cultivate the activities that make you feel secure in the here and now.

The Third House

The Third House relates to all issues connected to the everyday use of your mind: what you tend to think about, how you communicate, and what occupies your mind. Third House activities are fueled by the desire to get the information that can improve your life; whether this is for educational or recreational reasons, the need is to be informed. How you go about figuring things out when you are puzzled by something is also revealed here. The Third House is also the house of siblings and your first relationships outside of mom and dad.

The Fourth House

The Fourth House is your need to establish a home for yourself—a sanctuary where you can drop all your cares of the world and just be. The sign on your Fourth House describes your attitude toward and need to create roots in your life. All family issues, from the conditioning of growing up in your family of origin, to your nuclear family that you create as an adult, are the concerns of the Fourth House. The Fourth House represents the personal foundations you create that support every other aspect of your life. This is also where you will live and create a family with the people in your life whom you feel closest to.

The Fifth House

All matters concerning the heart are activated in the Fifth House. This house also describes what fun and play mean to you, and your approach to children, romance, entertainment, and creative expression—how you pour your heart into whatever you do. The Fifth House awakens the need for recreation, celebration, joy, laughter, and songs from the heart. Since romance is a Fifth House issue, this area is of vital importance for relationship astrology. There is more to a meaningful relationship than romance, but it sure adds a spark that is obviously missing when it is not there. If your relationship lacks romance, look to your own Fifth House to see how to unlock the expressive energy of romance.

The Sixth House

At first glance, the Sixth House of work, health, and daily routines doesn't seem to be involved much with relationships. It is also the house of all unequal relationships, as with employees or people you hire for services.

Can you care for yourself in a gentler way? I like the attitude of caring for your body as if it were a pet of yours. If you treated your body with the same loving care as you would for a pet, you would be a master of your Sixth House and would manifest relationships that were more supportive.

The Sixth House also governs your daily schedule and should not be understated in its ultimate impact on your life and relationships. If you have a picture of your ideal life, and yet the ingredients are not there in the daily life that would lead to this ideal, how could you make it come about? There is your Sixth House homework: get more control over your daily schedule so that day by day, you are moving step-by-step toward your ideal life. In relationships, creating a daily schedule that blends with your partner helps.

The Seventh House

The Seventh House is most commonly called the house of relationships and is where you learn about yourself reflected through the other people in your life. We call the Seventh the House of Relationships as if it were a noun, but the Seventh House could more accurately be described as a process. We also call this the house of agreements, but then it necessarily involves disagreements, and specifically the process of bringing agreement to disagreement. This is the art of negotiation: the diplomacy of never settling for less than what is in your best interests, nor demanding more than what is fair. Making agreements, for any reason, that do not honor the self, never lead to anything worthwhile.

Planets in your Seventh House need involvements with others to get activated. You can't do your Seventh House alone—it represents your shared experiences.

The Eighth House

The Eighth House is the house of sex, death, and shared resources. The Eighth House is where you go through the deeper transformations that come from having an intimate relationship, or not. Yes, the underlying need of the Eighth House is to undergo such a deep transformation with your partner that both of you are changed in ways neither could have done by yourselves, but the Eighth House is also the repository of all the memories of every time you've ever been hurt, stepped on, cheated, done wrong, and abandoned. Thus, the work of the Eighth House is to keep the heart open so the armor from old wounds won't block the need for intimacy.

The Ninth House

The Ninth House is your need to reach beyond the introspective world of the Eighth House and engage in the opportunities for growth and expansion available to you. It is the house of travel, all things foreign and ethnic, higher education, philosophy, politics, and all opportunities to expand beyond your current reality. It is where you take the experiences of your Eighth House and generalize them into larger truths, applicable to the entire world around you. It is a transition house, from the relationship quadrant to the social quadrant. This is where you form your beliefs that will be your operating system for how you relate to the larger world. It is where you need to feel connected to your partner's ethics and philosophical outlook on life. It is where you can take part in activities with your partner to expand the world of your experience together.

The Tenth House

The Tenth House is your house of aspirations, particularly concerning career and professional and social goals. If you aspire to something that is in your best interests, and this dovetails with that which is the public's best interests, you experience the honor and the notoriety of the Tenth House. Thus, it represents your public standing and reputation. This house reveals your capacity to achieve and sustain success. In relationships, this drive for success can compete with the time it takes to have healthy relationships, so balance is required.

The Eleventh House

The Eleventh House is where you need to continue to expand the scope of your social involvement through friendships, your social life, and participation in groups and organizations that have social service at heart. This is where the "I" becomes "We," and this participation with "We" gives you a sense of belonging. This house also reveals your capacity to have friendships and how important they are to you. Social causes, political activism, and volunteering for community action are all ways of participating in the Eleventh House.

The Twelfth House

In many ways the Twelfth House is the most mysterious and hard to understand of all the houses. It is where you are meant to stand back from the world and contemplate its meaning. The inner world holds prominence with the Twelfth House. It reveals who you are behind the scenes, in the dark. This is the house of spirituality, as the separate ego identity is meant to dissolve in the Twelfth as you become aware of larger realities and the fact that there is more going on than meets the eye. This is the interface between you and the informing guides, saints, deities, or angels that you believe in. The Twelfth House is where you begin to understand spiritual law and how it manifests as karma in your life. The hidden realm of dreams also comes to life in the Twelfth House.

4
The Aspects—
How Your Characters Support
or Challenge Each Other

In our analogy of your chart representing the play of your life, the aspects reveal how the characters in their roles either support each other, or are in conflict. Technically, the aspects are the geometric relationships the planets make to one another, either within your chart, or between two individual's charts.

The aspects are specific points in a cycle that two planets are making with each other; some are harmonious and supportive of each other, while others challenge each other and often stir up conflict. Try to avoid thinking of the harmonious aspects as good and the challenging aspects as bad; since they both exist, you'll want to know how to work with both types of energy. There would be no energy and no action with only harmonious aspects, and there would be no peace with only challenging aspects. Can you enjoy the ease of the harmonious aspects without becoming lazy? Can you initiate action with the challenging aspects without it seeming like a battle? This is the dance of energy we all work with in dealing with the aspects.

♂ The Conjunction: 0°

Orb: + or – 10° for Sun and Moon, and 8° for all other planets.

Keywords: Blending and birthing.

When two or more planets are conjunct, there is a blending of their energies, and something is born from the union. Take the key themes of each planet and blend phrases together using keywords for both planets, and you'll get the meaning. The conjunction leads to a spontaneous eruption of life. When comparing two people's charts, conjunctions between each other's planets will always be hot spots in the relationship—events will happen here.

✱ The Sextile: 60°

Orb: + or – 6° for Sun and Moon, and 4° for all other planets.

Keywords: Creative flow.

The sextile is basically every other sign through the zodiac and is one of the most favorable aspects. There is natural harmony, with creative inspiration flowing between the two planets like a mild current of excitement. Planets in sextile to each other support and stimulate each other, and creatively work together.

◻ The Square: 90°

Orb: + or – 8° for Sun and Moon, and 6° for all other planets.

Keywords: Challenges, tension, frustration, anger, action.

The square is traditionally thought of as a hard aspect and it is even fair to call it difficult, and certainly challenging. When planets are in square aspect, they are working at cross-purpose to each other; the needs of one are in natural conflict with the needs of the other. Squares are first felt as anger, irritation, and frustration. This dynamic energy can be redirected into healthy activity if you can overcome the negative reaction.

△ The Trine: 120°

Orb: + or – 8° for Sun and Moon, and 6° for all other planets.

Keywords: Harmony, support.

Planets in trine aspect to each another are typically in the same element and thus in natural harmony with one another, which leads to comfort and ease between the two planets. Trines are great, but not necessarily as great as they might be unless you suc-

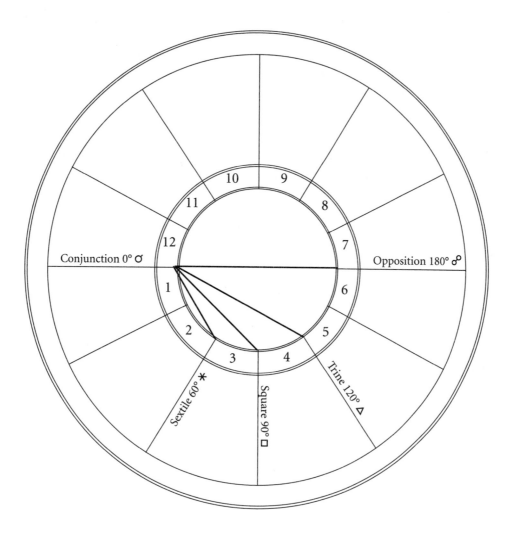

Chart 1
The Five Major Aspects

cessfully direct energy toward them; otherwise, they exist as passive harmony. The problem with the trine is that it is not a problem. We are a squeaky wheel type of culture and tend to focus on the challenges in front of us. The trine is not a challenge and can go by unnoticed. You have to direct energy toward it to get the benefits; otherwise, the planets will just be at ease with each other. With trines between charts, the planets will be naturally supportive of one another, as if they were working for the same cause.

☍ The Opposition: 180°

Orb: + or − 10° for Sun and Moon, and 8° for all other planets.

Keywords: Competition, or cooperation.

The opposition is right up there with the conjunction in terms of strength of impact. In the conjunction, the planetary energies are fused together, while in the opposition, they present themselves as polar opposites. At first, the opposition presents itself as "you and your opponent." With experience, you begin to recognize this as two distinct and separate views of life within yourself, and then you can start benefiting from this aspect by seeing both sides of every issue. Until it is integrated, the opposition presents itself as difficulties with others. It seems as if the world is picking on you; someone is always there to take issue with your perspective. This goes on until you accept it as normal and even expect the opposing view. Then you are enriched by opposing views, rather than threatened by them; you learn to dance with the polarity, rather than trying to ultimately have one be right and the other wrong.

Sign	House	Planet	Element	Mode
Aries	First	Mars	Fire	Cardinal
Taurus	Second	Venus	Earth	Fixed
Gemini	Third	Mercury	Air	Mutable
Cancer	Fourth	Moon	Water	Cardinal
Leo	Fifth	Sun	Fire	Fixed
Virgo	Sixth	Mercury	Earth	Mutable
Libra	Seventh	Venus	Air	Cardinal
Scorpio	Eighth	Pluto	Water	Fixed
Sagittarius	Ninth	Jupiter	Fire	Mutable
Capricorn	Tenth	Saturn	Earth	Cardinal
Aquarius	Eleventh	Uranus	Air	Fixed
Pisces	Twelfth	Neptune	Water	Mutable

Part Two
Your Relationship Profile

It is tempting to think that if you find the right partner who has all of the right astrological combinations, then all of your relationship issues will be solved. It doesn't work that way. You would still be the same you, with your same chart, and with the same issues that have always been with you. Rather than wait for that perfect match, it is far more valuable for you to fully understand your relationship profile: your strengths, needs, challenges, and fears, considering all of the astrological factors in your chart that impact your relationships. Then, at least, while you are waiting for that perfect match, your efforts to better understand yourself will definitely improve your capacity to enjoy your existing relationships.

Your chart holds valuable clues as to the skills and challenges that you bring to any relationship. Your chart is a map to the territory you enter into when you get involved in relationships. Like the saying "Healer, first heal thyself," astrologer, first know yourself; know your own chart and what gets activated in relationships, regardless of whom you are with.

5
Exploring the Relationship Houses

Note: The sign on the cusp of a house describes your attitude of approach to the matters concerning the particular house.

Example: A chart has Aries on the Fifth House cusp, Gemini on the Seventh House cusp, and Cancer on the Eighth House cusp. Aries on the Fifth describes a person who approaches matters of the heart with enthusiasm, spontaneity, and a need for excitement. Gemini on the Seventh would lead to a highly mental approach to the house of relationships, with a strong need for communication. And Cancer on the Eighth would approach intimacy with caution and then find great nurturing in a deeply intimate relationship.

Note: If there are planets in the house in question, they will bring themes consistent with the planet into the house in question.

Example: If you have Mars in the Seventh House, you will need a partner who can handle the power, passion, and intensity that gets activated in your relationship house.

Taking It Further

- The ruling planet of a house is the planet associated with the sign on the cusp of the house.
- The ruling planet is creating experiences through its sign, house, and aspects, which will impact the house in question.
- The sign of the ruling planet is a subdominant attitude that has bearing on the matters concerning the house in question.
- The house of the ruling planet will be tied in an influential way to the house in question.
- Aspects between the ruling planet and other planets will pull these other planets and their houses into the scenario.

Taking It Even Further

- Planets in a house will draw experiences to the house based on the conditions of planets involved.
- Aspects from other planets to planets in a particular house will have a direct bearing on situations involving that area of life. Are the aspects supportive or challenging? The houses these aspecting planets occupy and their concerns also get pulled into the mix.
- Look to the sign that any planet in a house naturally rules for further clues. For example, if Mars is in a house in question, where is Aries in the chart?
- Finally, which planet is the natural ruler of the house in question? Its sign, house, and aspects will complete the picture.

6
The Sun Through
the Houses and Signs

Note: Space doesn't permit a separate exploration for both the signs and houses. In this presentation we are linking them together, so read both the sign placement and the house placement. Consider the sign as the dominant theme and the house as a subdominant theme.

Sun in Aries or the First House

You thrive in a relationship that allows for your fiery, enthusiastic nature. You are action-oriented and need a partner who can keep up with your pace. You can handle challenges and thrive on excitement, but you don't handle the status quo or routines well—too boring! Keep your relationship vital by always keeping something new on the horizon to explore together. You need to develop patience with other people's slower pace, and also your listening skills, to improve your relationships.

Sun in Taurus or the Second House

You are a connoisseur of quality and like nice possessions; thus your earthy nature thrives in a relationship that is secure and stable, and provides abundance. You are a comfort seeker and are affectionate by nature, so a snuggly, comfortable relationship is to your liking. You prefer real and genuine as qualities in a partner more than flashy and ostentatious. To improve your relationships, you need to cultivate flexibility in your ability to accept other people's values.

Sun in Gemini or the Third House

Your bright, intellectual nature thrives in a relationship that feeds your mind—it is important for you to stay fascinated by life in general, or you get bored. You are empowered by communication and the flow of ideas, as well as a life with much variety, and will do best in a relationship that stimulates you in these ways. Your mind can think anything and this can be hugely distracting in relationships; thus you need to cultivate the ability to drop out of your mind and into your emotions to improve your relationships.

Sun in Cancer or the Fourth House

Your watery nature thrives in a relationship in which you feel a deep emotional connection. It is imperative for you to be able to feel what your partner is going through—you would shrivel up with a partner who shut you out from his or her emotional feelings. The personal side of life is what you are most interested in sharing. You need someone who receives your nurturing energy without becoming co-dependent. You could work on your tendency to take everything so personally that it makes it difficult to carry on sensitive conversations with others.

Sun in Leo or the Fifth House

Your fiery, dramatic nature thrives in a relationship that is heartful, playful, and fun loving. You also need to be the center of attention in your partner's life. Ideally, you will give back as much as you demand, but with Leo, you are meant to reach for the gold and expect a lot out of life. "Follow your heart" is good advice for anyone, but for Leo it is law. You need a relationship with plenty of heart. You could improve your relationships by learning how to step outside of your own perspective and look at your relationship through your partner's eyes.

Sun in Virgo or the Sixth House

You are down to earth and practical, and need to be in a relationship with someone who appreciates these qualities. You feel comfortable with someone who appreciates your qualities of genuineness and sincerity. You like to be of service and helpful and would thrive in a relationship with someone with whom you could build a life together, shoulder to shoulder, from the ground up. You need to be with someone who appreciates your eye for detail and doesn't think you are just being picky. To improve your relationships, you could work on your tendency to analyze everything, which takes you out of your heart.

Sun in Libra or the Seventh House

Your airy nature thrives in a relationship with much communication and cooperation in most endeavors; you want to do things together. You would appreciate a partner who appreciates the refinements of life, like culture and the arts. You appreciate elegance and eloquence in your relationships. You crave harmony and shy away from the unpleasant. You could improve your relationships by working on your tendency to settle for peace at any cost, and raising the standard by learning to negotiate an honorable agreement for both of you.

Sun in Scorpio or the Eighth House

Your emotionally intense nature would thrive in a relationship that brings out your passion. You have a private side of your character that needs to be honored. It's not that you have anything to hide; you just feel better with some privacy in your life. Your vulnerability deals with trust/mistrust issues, which arise in relationships. Because of this vulnerability, you need to be with someone you trust completely. You could improve your relationships by learning how to resist your tendency to pull back from a relationship in silent resentment—these buried grudges and wounds create a gulf between you and the person you want to be closest to. Learn to deal with issues as they arise, learn what can be learned, and then move on with an open heart.

Sun in Sagittarius or the Ninth House

Your fiery, outgoing nature would thrive in a relationship that embraces your "life as an adventure" attitude. You are at your best when you are living life as if it were a quest. You would thrive in a positive relationship that is open to exploring, traveling, and expanding the mind and soul. Finding a partner who shares your interest in higher education and philosophy would be ideal. To improve your relationships, you could work on cultivating patience and toning down your tendency to moralize.

Sun in Capricorn or the Tenth House

Your earthy nature would thrive in a relationship committed to building a life together. You are a builder and have the patience and determination to bring your plans into manifest form. Sincere, loyal, and genuine are the qualities that you would like to be appreciated for. You could work on lightening up on your ambitions. Although you need someone to appreciate your naturally serious disposition, it would be ideal to be in a relationship with someone who can get you out of your "all work and no play" routine.

Sun in Aquarius or the Eleventh House

Your airy temperament would thrive in a relationship that is strong on the mental and friendship qualities. You seek the unusual and unique, and need to be with someone who appreciates your ability to think outside of the box. You need more freedom than most in a relationship and will grant that same freedom to those you share with. When your independent streak is out of line, you can look at anything requiring cooperation as a threat to your independence. Then it is important to remember that independence and commitment are not mutually exclusive: you can get involved in commitment-based relationships in a way that is authentic to you.

Sun in Pisces or the Twelfth House

Your watery, sensitive nature would thrive in a relationship that is deeply interactive, particularly on an emotional level. You are the incurable romantic and do best in a relationship that allows for your imaginative, compassionate nature to express itself. You don't hold back in love, and if you want to improve your relationships, learn to hold back a little bit. When you totally surrender to the needs of your partner to the point of sacrificing your own needs, the well runs dry and you have less to give. You also need quality time alone, on a regular basis, to stay in your center.

7
Sun Aspects in Your Chart

Is the Sun in your birth chart well aspected, suggesting strong self-esteem to bring into relationships? Or is it challenged, suggesting a lack of confidence and self-esteem, which will be brought into the relationship? The Sun's aspects to the Moon are particularly important, as they set unconscious patterns of expectation as to whether relationships will be harmonious or in conflict.

For our purposes in this book, we will group the harmonious and challenging aspects together. The conjunction is most often treated separately, but grouped with the harmonious or challenging aspects when appropriate. Read the definitions below and then look up your specific aspect on the following pages to fine-tune your interpretation.

Harmonious aspects: Sextile and trine (and sometimes the conjunction).
Challenging aspects: Square and opposition (and sometimes the conjunction).

Sun to Moon

Conjunction

With the Sun and Moon fused together, you would benefit from a relationship that adds the missing objectivity that you need to better understand yourself. You don't need someone just like you; you already have enough of that.

Harmonious

The masculine/feminine energies in your personality flow together quite naturally, and you expect to feel at ease in relationships.

Challenging

The masculine/feminine energies are in conflict within your personality, and you tend to have the unconscious expectation that your relationships will be stressful. You need a relationship with someone who diffuses your tension.

Sun to Mercury

Conjunction

You are articulate and naturally expressive as a communicator. However, you tend to think too much about yourself and could benefit from having a partner who pulls you out of excessive self-reflection.

> *Note:* Mercury always stays close to the Sun throughout the zodiac, so the conjunction is the only major aspect that is possible in a birth chart.

We can look at which planet rises first in your chart for more clues about relationships. Locate both the Sun and Mercury in your chart, and imagine them both moving at equidistance in a clockwise direction through your chart. Which one crosses your Ascendant, and thus rises, first? Mercury or the Sun?

Mercury Rising Ahead of the Sun

Your mind loves to anticipate and plan for what is going to happen. You tend to make snap decisions, sometimes before all of the relevant information is in. With your mind racing out in front of your experience, you like to talk about ideas and possibilities.

Mercury Rising After the Sun

Your mind likes to wait for the experience until you form your opinions. You prefer to discuss that which is real to you, that which you have personally experienced, as opposed to abstract possibilities that have no personal bearing on your life.

Sun to Venus

Conjunction

Love, romance, and affection are natural for you. You need a partner who can celebrate your naturally loving nature without catering to your indulgent side.

> *Note:* Venus always stays close to the Sun throughout the zodiac, so the conjunction is the only major aspect that is possible in a birth chart.

We can look at which planet rises first in your chart for more clues about relationships. Locate the Sun and Venus in your chart, and imagine them both moving at equidistance in a clockwise direction through your chart. Which one crosses your Ascendant, and thus rises, first? Venus or the Sun?

Venus Rising Before the Sun

Venus anticipates pleasure before the actual experience when it rises before the Sun, thus some of the joy is in anticipating the pleasure. This keeps you open to possibilities, and makes you more gullible. You sometimes make value judgments before all of the information is in.

Venus Rising After the Sun

Venus wants to wait and see what the experience is before it gets excited when it rises after the Sun. This wait-and-see attitude makes you less gullible and slower to rise toward excitement on the one hand, and able to linger in enjoyable experiences without rushing off to something new on the other.

Sun to Mars

Conjunction

Your passionate warrior energy is fused with your self-identity. You need a partner who can handle your intense energy and help you direct your power into constructive activities.

Harmonious

You have a natural confidence that lets you know you will be able to handle whatever comes your way. This gives you courage in love, and in life.

Challenging

You tend to feel picked on, as if the world were badgering you and looking for a fight. You need a partner who doesn't bite on your defensive tendencies and can roll with the punches.

Sun to Jupiter

Harmonious (including conjunction)

Confidence comes easily to you, and you assume life will be a rewarding experience. You expect a lot out of life and need a partner who can appreciate your natural generosity.

Challenging

With your tendency toward excessiveness, you would benefit from a partner who can help you *not* over-give, over-do, and generally expect more than what is available.

Sun to Saturn

Harmonious

With your patient, persevering nature, you look for a long-term, commitment-based relationship. You are not threatened by a relationship's periodic challenges and have the patience to work through the difficulties that beset any relationship.

Challenging (including conjunction)

You tend to expect the worst in most situations and need a partner who can help you maintain a positive self-image. You tend to attract the voice of disapproval in a partner, echoing a childhood pattern, but that is not what you need.

Sun to Uranus

Harmonious (including conjunction)

You accept your uniqueness and that of others. "Don't judge me; I won't judge you" tends to be your attitude. You thrive in relationships that continue to grow and evolve.

Challenging

You tend to fight for your right to be free and independent. You may either attract people who have difficulty making commitments, or become the one who feels threatened by commitment. You would benefit from a relationship with someone who helps you see that independence and commitment are not mutually exclusive.

Sun to Neptune

Harmonious

It is fairly easy for you to transcend the petty and see the bigger picture. You would benefit from being with a partner who appreciates your refined temperament and shares your creative and spiritual interests.

Challenging

Your imagination causes you more trouble than good until you get a handle on this challenge. At the highest level we could say you are going through a spiritual crisis in this life—your soul will not let you find complete fulfillment in the world until you have come to spiritual reconciliation within yourself. Until then, watch out for the blind spots this aspect is known for, particularly the tendency to get involved in savior/victim types of relationships.

Sun to Pluto

Conjunction

The compelling drive of Pluto is merged with the self-identity of the Sun in your personality, giving you power times two. You are being tested with the right use of power that comes from your ability to influence others. With this power, you can always stay in control, but then you miss out on so much of life that happens when you are not in control. You need a partner who is strong enough to stand up to your controlling ways.

Harmonious

You are at ease in most situations and rarely feel threatened, as if you had a deep strength to draw on. You are able to use power without drawing undue attention to yourself; thus you are a natural in leadership roles.

Challenging

Control/surrender games enter into most of your relationships. Is it the power of love, or the love of power, that drives your choices? You need a partner who can love you through your desperation, and into the arms of safety.

Sun to the North Node

Harmonious (including conjunction)

You tend to naturally move toward that which is growth-oriented for your soul and in your best interests.

Challenging

You tend to get pulled to the path of least resistance and need a partner who is not indulgent in this way.

Sun to the South Node

Conjunction

This combination leads to a unique set of interpretive circumstances. Typically, we think of the South Node as a place where you wouldn't expect growth; familiarity, but not growth. However, we would never advise someone to move away from the Sun. Therefore, for you there is still growth through the past, be it past lives, or past relationships in this life. Still, there are likely certain attributes about your Sun sign that are not growth-oriented for you at all.

Harmonious

You are able to align with your past without getting hooked into it. You draw from the lessons already learned.

Challenging

You tend toward a life of one step forward and two steps back. It would be beneficial to work on changing that to two steps forward and one step back.

8
The Moon Through the Houses and Signs

Moon in Aries or the First House

Your emotional nature is fiery and intense and you are proud of it! You would do best in a relationship that allows for your intensity. You respond to your emotions in the moment, making the timid shy away from you, but the right partner enjoys your independent nature and love of spontaneous emotional expression. You don't let things lie around and fester; there is a sense of urgency about your emotions and you need to clear the air now. You do best with a partner who doesn't try to repress or control your instinctive nature. Too much routine is not good for you; you get restless and impatient, so plan a life that has much room for spontaneous pursuits.

Moon in Taurus or the Second House

Your earthy emotional nature requires a relationship with stability and security as core themes in order for you to be at your best. You feel more comfortable with people who are real and genuine and are ill at ease with those who are too flighty; if there is nothing for you to depend on, there is no Taurus hook. Trust is absolutely essential in your relationships to bring out your nurturing qualities, and your love is long lasting. Your emotions are soothed in a healthy, affectionate relationship. You will seek to be helpful for your partner, and appreciation for this is essential, or resentments could form.

Moon in Gemini or the Third House

With your emotional nature in an air sign, you are more comfortable in your mind, thinking and talking about emotions, as opposed to lingering in the deep, felt emotions themselves. This is your emotional style and you would flourish in a relationship with someone who also has an airy emotional disposition or, at minimum, someone who is not prone to prolonged moods. This would be oppressive to your emotional nature, like you were stuck underwater and needed to come up for air. You need to be with a partner who can talk through emotional issues with you and then move on—there are too many interesting things for Gemini to explore to get stuck on something along the way.

Moon in Cancer or the Fourth House

You need to feel the emotional closeness of family to be at your best in a relationship. You need to be with a partner who understands your cautious nature and honors it. You are slow to trust someone with your deepest sensitivities, but once you let someone into your circle of trust, you become the most loyal and attached partner of all. You are a nurturer and need a relationship that allows for this up-close-and-personal need to be at your best. You need to be with a partner who understands that emotions are not a disease! They are a vital source of nurturing and loving energy that you invest your whole self in.

Moon in Leo or the Fifth House

You need room to express your dramatic emotional nature in love. You put your heart in your emotional expression and thrive in a relationship where the heartfelt connection is dominant. Your fun-loving disposition can't handle being with someone who is too serious; you are at your best with someone with whom you can laugh, kick up your heels, and find creative ways to explore life together. You are dramatic and strong in your emotional expression and need someone who is strong enough not to be intimidated by this show of strength.

Moon in Virgo or the Sixth House

Your down-to-earth emotional nature is most comfortable with someone who fits with your day-to-day routines. You are not looking for a dramatic, weekend-fling type of romance; you are more comfortable in a relationship where you are involved in each other's day-to-day life. For you, downtime is just another type of busy time, and you would be at your best with a partner who also enjoys this task-oriented approach to life. You can hold yourself back with overcautious, critical analysis of yourself and would do well in a relationship with a partner who lets go of it and moves on when an issue has been analyzed to death. Warm and gushy don't come natural to you, but sincere and genuine do, and you will be most comfortable with someone who appreciates your mental approach to emotions. When at ease, you are bright and clever in the way you naturally express yourself.

Moon in Libra or the Seventh House

Your Moon in an air sign shows you are most comfortable in a relationship that doesn't have much emotional trauma and drama. You are at your best when things stay even keeled, and you thrive in a relationship with a great deal of mental interaction. Your refined emotional disposition shies away from coarse and vulgar behavior, and you appreciate a partner with some refinement of character. You will want to talk through all important decisions with your partner and need time to consider issues from all sides before you are comfortable acting. You strive to please and would be at your best with a partner who doesn't take advantage of this.

Moon in Scorpio or the Eighth House

Your passionate emotional nature flourishes in a relationship built on trust, but takes a nose-dive when mistrust is dominant—trust is that important to you. Sexuality is also important to you and, in a healthy relationship, is an important form of emotional bonding and healing. You crave an emotional intimacy beyond sex; you long to emotionally merge with another to such a degree that there is no trace of separateness. This is the treasure, but it is guarded by all the armor that comes from every time you have been wounded, cheated on, stepped on, lied to, and abandoned. These are the most difficult experiences we go through in relationships, and their memories are stored with the attitude of "Never forgive and never forget." This unfortunate attitude locks you into the past experience. The high road is the emotional work it takes to keep your heart open. If you are willing to confront the hidden side of your own psyche to search for clues of what you need to work on when problems erupt, you will go through the deep transformations and growth that keep the heart open.

Moon in Sagittarius or the Ninth House

Your upbeat emotional nature thrives in a positive relationship with plenty of activity. Your emotional enthusiasm needs room to express itself by reaching out and taking a big bite out of life. The higher-mind topics of philosophy and religion are likely important to you, and you would like a partner who enjoys travel and educational pursuits, with plenty of play. You live by your principles and high ethical standards, which is, of course, favorable. But when this comes off as self-righteous, you've gone too far and others may perceive you as dogmatic and moralistic. You prefer the honest, blunt approach to dealing with emotional issues and get impatient with people who are indirect and don't say what they really mean.

Moon in Capricorn or the Tenth House

Your rather serious emotional nature thrives in a project-oriented relationship with a strong basis of loyalty and commitment. You are a builder and an organizer and are at your best with a partner who shares your ambitions. Your love commitments are long lasting, so choose wisely. You would definitely appreciate a partner who fits into the system of order that you need for comfort, but you would also definitely benefit from a partner who gets you out of your work mode once in a while to appreciate the other dimensions of a relationship. You are comfortable in roles of responsibility, and others defer to your natural leadership. Professionally, this is an advantage, but in your personal life it is a handicap. You can appear so confident as to not have any needs from others whatsoever. So when you need some tender-loving care and understanding, other people don't see that at all until you learn to reveal your sensitivities, at least to your partner.

Moon in Aquarius or the Eleventh House

You are an emotionally free-spirited soul who has the strength to stand by your convictions when you differ from the crowd. You need a lot of space in a relationship to honor your sense of independence, and you will grant that same freedom to your partner. You wouldn't do well in a clinging-vine type of relationship; you respect independence in others as well. You explore your emotions through your mind and need a partner who can talk through the issues with you. You are emotionally fed by maintaining your friendships, and the friendship level of a love relationship needs to stay vital to hold your interest. There is a bit of the rebel in you; you like to have something in your life to rebel against—don't let it be your relationship! You would also value a partner who doesn't mind throwing out the rule book for relationships and going it your own way together.

Moon in Pisces or the Twelfth House

This is the most sensitive placement of all for the Moon, showing you to be a person who feels everything. You need to be in a relationship with someone who supports your emotional sensitivity and periodic need for quality time alone. You are not just being moody; the two fish of Pisces tell the story: one in the outer world like everyone else, and one in the inner world that only you and God know about. How skilled you are at moving between these two realms makes all the difference. You are tremendously compassionate and prone to be pulled into the suffering you feel around you; thus you would benefit from a partner who can help you release these emotions. Pisces is an incurable romantic, and you would love a relationship that caters to your romantic nature. You are probably not skilled at defining emotional boundaries, and the wrong partner could take advantage of your self-sacrificing tendencies, so choose wisely.

9
Moon Aspects
in Your Chart

Is the Moon in your birth chart well aspected, suggesting emotional confidence in deal-ing with the needs of a relationship? Or is it challenged, suggesting a fear of being over-whelmed by the emotional demands of a relationship?

Moon to Mercury

Conjunction

Your mind is strongly influenced by your emotions. You can articulate your emotions, but it is hard to tell whether you feel that you think something, or you think that you feel something. It would be ideal for you to be in a relationship with someone who helps you distinguish between your thoughts and your emotions.

Harmonious

You have a natural ability to communicate emotional issues effectively. The poet and the romantic would both benefit by being able to articulate emotions creatively, but all per-sonal relationships would also benefit from this combination.

Challenging

Your emotions are often at odds with your mind; thus people tend to misunderstand you when you are communicating emotional issues. It is not *what* you are saying that is the problem; it is more often *how* you are saying it that leads to misinterpretation. This can lead to rational arguments over emotional issues—always ludicrous at best. As you become aware of this discrepancy between your head and your heart, difficulty in emotional communication with others subsides.

Moon to Venus

Conjunction

This aspect leads to a loving, affectionate nature. You have a kind and gentle personality with a natural love of people.

Harmonious

Your natural emotional responses and habit patterns support what you value in relationships and how you receive love.

Challenging

This aspect manifests as a difficulty in being gracious when receiving compliments, gifts, return favors, or opportunities for assistance. Even asking for assistance is awkward, but this attitude also cuts off the flow of life and love coming to you. You would benefit by working on expanding what you allow yourself to receive. Work on choking out "Thank you, how kind!" when life is offering something to you.

Moon to Mars

Conjunction

Your emotions are fueled by the power, passion, and temper of Mars. This gives you emotional strength, though sometimes too much. You tend to run hot and need healthy outlets for your passions; otherwise, your emotional intensity can overwhelm others.

Harmonious

You have natural emotional courage. You are able to act on what you feel and can define your boundaries when need be, and have the ability to do this without provoking negative reactions in others. This makes you very comfortable in emotional relationships, with the confidence of knowing you can take care of yourself.

Challenging

Your emotional nature is often at odds with your warrior nature, making you appear more defensive than you feel. Your emotions run hot, and you need healthy outlets for your passionate, competitive nature; otherwise, your emotional intensity can feel hostile to others.

Moon to Jupiter

Harmonious (including conjunction)

You are naturally buoyant in your emotions; nothing keeps you down as you eventually frame most everything in a positive light. You are naturally generous to others, providing them with positive emotional support.

Challenging

Jupiter challenges lead to excess. With your Moon, this leads to excessive emotional responses; you tend to overreact to emotional situations. You can be inappropriately generous, and by giving too much, you create an imbalance in the giving and receiving in your relationships. Or you could grasp for more and more of a good thing, another form of excessiveness. Learn to spend more time in appreciation when you've got it good.

Moon to Saturn

Harmonious

With the best of Saturn, you get patience, perseverance, and determination. These qualities will all benefit your emotional nature, giving you patience in dealing with emotional issues, within yourself and with others. You can create a balanced life, with time for responsibilities and time for your personal life.

Challenging (including conjunction)

Challenges from Saturn restrict. With your Moon, this leads to choked-off emotional expression. It is not easy to flow with situations, because you feel burdened and pressured by other people's expectations of you. There were likely circumstances in your early life that made emotional expression seem threatening. This leads to "emotional constipation" until you reclaim your authority over your emotional life. Then, the fear of disapproval will subside, leading to easier emotional relationships.

Moon to Uranus

Conjunction

Your emotional nature is highly original and very exciting. Your independent streak will certainly color your relationships and shows that you would thrive in an open relationship with room for each other's individuality. Your temperament is often erratic, though always original. You need a relationship that allows for this; otherwise, you will feel constrained, like you are going to jump out of your skin.

Harmonious

Your talent is your innovative ability to respond to emotional situations as the need presents itself. You rarely feel stuck or blocked. You are not threatened by differing opinions or views, and this lack of defensiveness allows your relationships considerable room for freedom of expression.

Challenging

Your need for freedom can interfere with your need for emotional stability. You rebel against any attempts to restrain or restrict you. You may have difficulties making commitments, or attract others to you who have difficulties with commitment, until you resolve this issue. Are independence and emotional commitment mutually exclusive? Or can you learn to honor your individuality while tending to the needs of an emotional relationship?

Moon to Neptune

Conjunction

This aspect leads to acute sensitivity in your emotional field. Neptune desires to transcend everyday emotional issues, which can lead to avoidance. Because of your compassionate nature, you could confuse relationships with savior/victim themes. The artist and the spiritual seeker can benefit the most from this aspect, aligning their imagination with that which inspires the emotional nature. But imagination can also lead to fear, escapism, excessive fantasy, and illusions upon illusions. Until you find a healthy connection to the imaginative, sensitive, and transcendent realm of Neptune, your emotional well-being is vulnerable to fear, escapism, and all types of illusions that come from undisciplined imagination.

Harmonious

Your ability to transcend petty issues and maintain your glowing emotional nature is a gift. You naturally use your imagination in a way that feeds your emotional nature positively. You are sustained by an inner faith that leads you to inner guidance.

Challenging

Your imagination often clouds and distorts your emotional experiences. This can lead to flights of fantasy, imagining how your life would be better if things were only different, and also to falling prey to the deception of others. Your imagination continues to cause you problems until you (1) discipline your imagination in either an artistic or spiritual activity, and (2) learn to compensate for emotional blind spots by making sure you've seen everything in full-case scenario, the possible best and the possible worst, before you get emotionally involved.

Moon to Pluto

Harmonious

Your ability to rejuvenate yourself emotionally after a wounding experience is a gift. You heal well, which allows you to stay emotionally open to intimacy. This also gives you a tremendous well of emotional strength to draw upon.

Challenging (including conjunction)

Your powerful emotional nature often keeps you in control of situations—and blocked from intimacy. It can feel threatening to surrender to emotional situations, and perhaps you have painful memories of why it is important to keep your guard up. But one way or another, power and control issues will dominate your emotional relationships until you learn to drop all intentions of influencing the outcomes of your closest relationships. Then, the magic of intimacy presents itself as life experiences you wouldn't have had if you were always in control.

Moon to the Nodes

Conjunction to South Node

Both the Moon and the South Node are pulls to the past, so this double emphasis often leads to emotional patterns that are deeply rooted in your experience with your family of origin and the patterns you brought with you into this life. Your life can become mired in family issues and in unsettled, unresolved issues from the past. This makes it doubly hard to pull out of the path of least resistance when you are trying to move forward in your life. Assume that there was something that you needed to learn from your family of origin, either in what was, or wasn't, provided. Accept the teaching, learn the lesson, and then move on.

Conjunction to North Node

Your emotional behavior patterns are perfectly aligned with your path of soul growth for this life. That which you need to nurture your personal emotional life is the same as that which you need for your soul growth.

Harmonious

Your emotional patterns naturally lead to, and support, your path of soul growth in this life. You accept the lessons that life has given you in the past and are involved in a growth-oriented lifestyle.

Square

The pulls from the past and the call to the future are equally strong and, at times, battling one other. You can have both resentments about your past and resistance toward your future growth. This can paralyze your growth until you learn to practice acceptance of your path.

10
The Ascendant/ Seventh House Cusp Through the Houses and Signs

Your Ascendant is another name for your rising sign and shows your attitude of approach to most situations. It is your orientation to life. Astrologer Kim Rogers-Gallagher calls your Ascendant your "front door" through which you go out into the world.[1] The opposite point in the chart from your Ascendant is your Seventh House cusp, which shows your attitude of approach to relationships and what you need brought out in you through others to complement your own perspective.

Aries Rising/Libra Seventh House

You approach life with great enthusiasm and drive. Your gut-level instincts serve you well in initiating the activities you need to maintain your self-interests. You know how to reach out and get what you need for your separate sense of self. With Libra on your Seventh House cusp, you need a partner who can help teach you how to be with others. Someone who can help you be aware of the needs of others in social situations would be

---

1. Kim Rogers-Gallagher, *Astrology for the Light Side of the Brain* (San Diego, CA: ACS Publications, 1995).

ideal. Maintaining your independence within cooperative relationships is the balancing act that will work for you.

Taurus Rising/Scorpio Seventh House

With Taurus rising, you know your personal values and want to build a life of quality and comfort in the material world. You approach life with a connoisseur's eye for quality, and you won't compromise on your values, which makes you very reliable, though a bit bull-headed at times. With Scorpio on your Seventh House cusp, you need a relationship with a partner who can awaken the emotional and passionate side of your character. It is very difficult for you at times to be with an emotionally complex person, but that is just what you need to get you out of your comfort zone and into the risky zone of shared emotional experiences, where growth and transformation can occur.

Gemini Rising/Sagittarius Seventh House

With Gemini rising, you have a flirtatious, playful personality and like to keep your options open. Your gift is communication and the ability to gather information you need to see your options from many perspectives. With Sagittarius on your Seventh House cusp, you need a partner who can keep you on track toward your goals. You need an upbeat, positive person in your life, someone you can get out and explore life together with.

Cancer Rising/Capricorn Seventh House

With Cancer rising, you are naturally loyal and nurturing to those you consider your family. Home, house, and family life are your priorities, and with Capricorn on the Seventh House cusp, you would benefit from a deeply committed relationship with a partner who can help you achieve your dreams. You are strong on the personal, and could benefit from a partner who encourages the professional side of your character.

Leo Rising/Aquarius Seventh House

With Leo rising, you project your heart and soul into everything you do, with great personal pride. You give creativity and fun high priority, and this gives you a ton of personality. With Aquarius on the Seventh House cusp, you need a relationship that helps you detach from your personal life and see the bigger picture. Your life partner also has to be your best friend.

Virgo Rising/Pisces Seventh House

With Virgo rising, you have an exquisite eye for detail and are naturally task-oriented in your approach to life. You like to keep your act together in all ways, and are at your best when engaged in some type of self-improvement program. This eases your self-critical eye, which is relentless when you are not doing something to improve yourself. With Pisces on the Seventh House cusp, you need a partner who takes you out of your perfectly manicured world and into the chaos of emotions and love. You are like dry earth yourself, and Pisces is the water that you need to make the garden fertile and to bring out the soft, loving side of your character.

Libra Rising/Aries Seventh House

With Libra rising, you project grace and style into the world. You are naturally considerate of other people's perspectives and seek harmony in most situations. This people-pleasing tendency can go too far when you compromise your values for the sake of peace. Then you have lost your strength and become a puppet to other people's expectations. With Aries on your Seventh House cusp, you need a fiery partner who can motivate you into action after you have considered all of the options for the umpteenth time.

Scorpio Rising/Taurus Eighth House

With Scorpio rising, you are passionate and intense in your orientation to life, but somewhat guarded and suspicious. You are shrewd, complex, and deep, making you appear mysterious and alluring to others. With Taurus on your Seventh House cusp, you need a partner who is down to earth, affectionate, and direct. Above all, you need a partner whom you trust completely. Being with someone who can help you enjoy the simple pleasures of life together would be ideal.

Sagittarius Rising/Gemini Seventh House

With Sagittarius rising, you approach life as if it were an adventure. You are a dreamer who seeks to inspire the dream in others. In your attempts to inspire others, you can unknowingly become dogmatic and evangelical. Thus, with Gemini on your Seventh

House cusp, you need a partner who has an open mind and who keeps you open-minded with intellectually stimulating discussions that help you see issues from other perspectives.

Capricorn Rising/Cancer Seventh House

With Capricorn rising, you project an aura of competence, dignity, and self-respect. This natural presentation of authority is great professionally, because you always look like you've got everything under control, but in your personal life, this is a handicap, because others don't know your emotional needs and sensitivities. Cancer on your Seventh House cusp indicates that you would benefit from a partner who sees through your strength and touches your emotional character. Being with someone who nurtures your personal life and family needs would be ideal.

Aquarius Rising/Leo Seventh House

With Aquarius rising, you approach life with some detachment in order to gain the far-ranging perspective for which you are known. Your unique perspective comes from seeing things outside of the box, and your views are sometimes shocking to those who still think inside the box. You need a partner who honors your radical, independent nature, and with Leo on the Seventh House cusp, a partner who awakens your heart and pulls you out of your mind would be ideal. You need a partner who knows how to have fun in life.

Pisces Rising/Virgo Eighth House

With Pisces rising, you approach life with compassion and emotional sensitivity. Your gift is your ability to stay open to the wonder of life; your downfall might very well come from this openness without discrimination. The downside would be playing the role of the self-sacrificing martyr, or being unable to separate yourself from the worries and concerns of others. With Virgo on your Seventh House cusp, you would benefit from a partner who helps you zero in on what is most important, organize your priorities, and become more effective in your life.

11
Mercury Through the Houses and Signs

What are the issues surrounding Mercury in your birth chart? How important is communication to you in relationships and what is your natural style of communication?

Mercury in Aries or the First House

The strength of your mind is in your independence and ability to think on your feet in the spontaneous moment. The best ideas of Aries are born in the moment and they arise within you. You thrive on new ideas and can interject inspiration for new activities to keep your relationships lively and interesting. You keep the air clear in a relationship by saying what needs to be said in the moment. To improve your relating skills, you could work on developing patience, particularly in allowing others to make decisions at their own pace, although developing patience as a listener would also be helpful.

Mercury in Taurus or the Second House

Your strength is in your common sense, your ability to see things as they really are, and your tenacity to follow through on projects. Your steady mind can help keep a relationship on track, particularly with issues concerning security and money. Mercury in Taurus does have the connoisseur's eye for quality and nice things. You have strong convictions and won't compromise your values, which is a strength in most situations. However, there are times when you are just being stubborn and resistant to the ideas of others. With this in mind, you could examine your resistances to see if they are really serving you or impeding the flow of your relationships.

Mercury in Gemini or the Third House

You have a gift for communicating, with your versatile, nonstop mind; you can find something interesting in everyone you meet. You are curious about everything, and with your love of variety, you can keep a relationship from ever becoming boring. You can be articulate with your own ideas, and genuinely interested in the ideas of others. You are at your best when coming up with new options, but are not so good at staying with one choice. You could improve your relationships by developing some focus to stay on the topic at hand in important discussions.

Mercury in Cancer or the Fourth House

Your mind is strongly influenced by your emotions, thus you are meant to *feel* your way through life, rather than think your way through. You also hear things at two levels: you hear the words, but you also hear the words not spoken . . . you feel the emotional content of the communication. You are a natural caregiver, but you need to feel considerable trust before you open up to others. You are skilled at getting people to talk about their personal lives. Cancer takes everything personally, and this will test your relationships. To improve your relating skills, you could work on pulling up out of your emotions, and focus on empathizing with what your partner is experiencing.

Mercury in Leo or the Fifth House

Your fiery, dramatic mind interjects a lot of fun and personality into your relationships. You know how to laugh and to get others to laugh, which makes your personality an asset in all that you do. Leo is at its best in a starring role, and you need a relationship with someone who pays considerable attention to your every word. This isn't arrogance; it is Leo and will bring out the best of your considerable personality. Leo, like all the fire signs, is very defensive, so you could improve your relating skills by truly trying to understand the other person's perspective in a disagreement.

Mercury in Virgo or the Sixth House

Mercury function best in this sign and house, and this placement gives you a strong, analytical, and task-oriented type of mind. You have an eye for detail and see what needs to be done in any given situation. This, plus your need to be of service, shows you to be a partner who likes to roll up your sleeves and give your partner a hand in tending to the maintenance of life. This placement is known for fretting over issues, so you will have to watch a tendency to worry. You need a partner who appreciates your discriminating eye and doesn't think you are just being critical.

Mercury in Libra or the Seventh House

Libra rules relationships, and your Mercury in this placement shows a mind naturally oriented toward the cooperative needs of a relationship. You are genuinely interested in your partner's perspective and value a relationship where both individuals share in the important decision making. Fairness is a must. You would like a relationship that is open to the Libra refinements of cultural and artistic exploration. You could improve your relating skills by standing tall for that which is fair, just, and honorable, and avoiding your tendency to settle for peace at any cost.

Mercury in Scorpio or the Eighth House

You have a steel-trap type of mind with an excellent bull-crap detector; you know in a heartbeat if someone is speaking from his or her truth or not. Intensely private at times, you prefer in-depth conversation to chitchat and would do best with a partner who doesn't always demand to know what you are thinking about. You can be shrewd with money and can help the relationship with your financial insights. Your insights into other people's motivations can also be helpful for your partner. To improve your relating skills, you could work on your tendency toward resentment. When issues aren't dealt with in a relationship, a gulf can form between you and the person you want to be closest to; so learn not to keep your hostilities buried, because they will just magnify and create trouble later on.

Mercury in Sagittarius or the Ninth House

Your enthusiastic mind reaches out to life as if it were a huge opportunity, giving you the ability to frame experiences in a positive light. Your happy-go-lucky outlook can be a source of positive inspiration for your partner, and you will certainly dream up many adventures for the relationship to keep it from stagnating. You would enjoy a relationship with shared interests in travel, education, and philosophical pursuits. To improve your relating skills, you could develop patience and respect for your partner's boundaries. You want to say "Yes" to every opportunity, and need to develop sensitivity for how your "yes saying" is impacting your partner.

Mercury in Capricorn or the Tenth House

Your serious, task-oriented mind is long on commitment and short on fun. You have a knack for organization and can help your partner get his or her life on track. You are a natural planner and builder and would do best with a partner who shares your ambitions. You are absolutely loyal and express yourself with sincerity more than personality. You could enhance your relating skills by stretching yourself to understand those whose priorities include the personal, emotional, and creative sides of life.

Mercury in Aquarius or the Eleventh House

With your highly original mind, you form your own unique worldview and are independent enough to follow though on your perspective as if things were exactly as you see them. You bring the quality of friendship into your relationships and stretch your friends' perspectives by challenging them to think for themselves. You could enhance your relating skills by avoiding your tendency to detach from the immediacy of the conversation you are in; your ability to detach from the moment and frame the experience in the big picture is indeed a gift, but it often pulls you out of the immediate situation in front of you.

Mercury in Pisces or the Twelfth House

Your highly imaginative and sensitive mind makes you a natural listener. Others feel it is safe to communicate with you, and that you will understand them. Your tendency is to become entwined in other people's lives to the degree that you carry their worries and feel their sorrows. This is both your gift and your problem. You could improve your relating skills by learning to separate yourself from others when getting involved is pulling you down. You need to maintain your own mental well-being by knowing when you need quality time alone to get in touch with your source for renewal.

12
Mercury Aspects in Your Chart

Mercury to Venus

Note: Mercury and Venus always stay close to the Sun, so the only major aspects they can make to each other in a birth chart are the conjunction and sextile.

Conjunction

This is the soul of the artist, the romantic; a mind that is drawn to love and beauty. This aspect gives a very open personality, and when you communicate, your love of life comes through. Other people tend to enjoy your company and want to spend time with you because of this.

Sextile

This aspect gives you a warm and engaging personality. Your mind and your values are in natural harmony, and you are a skillful communicator in relationships. You don't just go through the motions in a relationship; you have creative ideas for enhancing and enjoying your connections with others.

Mercury to Mars

Conjunction

You have a strong, passionate, and intense mind. You approach mental pursuits aggressively and have the courage to act on your ideas. You can overwhelm timid partners, as you tend to come on strong with Mars backing up your words. You need a partner who can appreciate your mental strength and not overreact. When you are not actively pursuing mental growth, you feel frustrated.

Harmonious

This aspect makes you an effective communicator. You are able to be strong without being pushy, and can define your boundaries without being rude. You tend to provoke cooperation rather than defensiveness in others, which makes it easier for you to get along with most anyone.

Challenging

Your mind and your will are sometimes at odds with each other, and you have likely felt picked on, or badgered, by others at various times in your life. This conflict within you manifests as conflicts in relationships where you attract someone who criticizes you or intimidates you. Conversely, you could become a hostile person with a chip on your shoulder. The test is to direct the mental intensity you feel into some worthy project. This gives motivation. Work on this drive within yourself and you will avoid the conflicts that arise when you try to change someone else's behavior. You get frustrated with other people all too easily. Remove judgment and work on self-control.

Mercury to Jupiter

Harmonious (including conjunction)

This aspect gives you a love of learning of all sorts, and is also very favorable for communication. You tend to look at life as a field of opportunities, and this allows you to stay upbeat and positive. You not only love to learn, you also enjoy teaching and sharing what you have learned. This allows you to maintain a positive disposition in your relationships; you look for the best in others.

Challenging

Challenges from Jupiter always deal with excess of one type or another. With Mercury, it is excesses with the mind: too much talking, too big of plans, planning for more than what can be achieved, promising more than you can deliver. All of these are self-created problems, which start off as something positive, but just go too far.

Mercury to Saturn

Conjunction

This aspect creates "serious mind syndrome"; your mind can't get away from the demanding pressure of Saturn. If you engage this pressure proactively, this can lead to all types of accomplishments in education or business; otherwise, the pressure can feel like a worrisome weight on your shoulders. This serious-mind syndrome impacts your relationships as well. Here, you make serious commitments and dedicate yourself to pursuing these commitments with dedication and perseverance. You need someone who appreciates your sincerity, but who also helps you lighten up and enjoy your personal life.

Harmonious

This aspect gives you the best of Saturn—patience and perseverance—in all mental pursuits. You also have the ability to learn from your mistakes in communication, so you rarely make the same mistake twice, thus improving your relationships through time. You have the tenacity to work through the difficult moments in a relationship without buckling under.

Challenging

This aspect can make you overly cautious in expressing yourself. Your early experiences in life probably didn't promote self-confidence, resulting in a fear of disapproval so strong that it restricts your freedom of expression. It is important to battle through this fear of failure or disapproval, or it will limit your belief in what is possible for you. Try to avoid investing in what others think of you, and instead internalize authority in your life and demonstrate some mental discipline.

Mercury to Uranus

Conjunction

Uranus speeds up whatever it touches, and you have a lightning-quick mind with this combination. This aspect is known for its spontaneous flashes of insight. The trouble is, the world around you doesn't operate at this same speed, and you can get frustrated in your attempts to be understood. If you can stay grounded during these electrical surges, you will be able to sustain the higher mental energy; otherwise, you will treat the flashes of increased mental energy as anxiety and seek to rid yourself of the energy.

Harmonious

Your intuitive mind and your logical mind work well together, giving you tremendous learning abilities. You can become a brilliant conversationalist, adding fresh insights to every conversation. Your highly original ideas have relevance to the moment. You also enjoy other people's unique qualities and are open to the highly original ideas of others.

Challenging

Your intuitive mind and your logical mind are at odds with each other. The spontaneous flashes of insight that you get are disruptive to what you are currently trying to do. Your independent streak can cause you some trouble when you are at the stage of "fighting for your right to be free." It is too easy to find views and opinions that you disagree with and feel you must challenge. You pass the test when you no longer need approval for, nor fear disapproval of, your highly original ideas. Deep breathing can literally help calm the anxiety that comes from this combination.

Mercury to Neptune

Conjunction

You have a dreamy, poetic, mystical, romantic mind that is even psychic at times. This sensitivity is best expressed in artistic and spiritual fields, where a highly imaginative mind is a benefit. However, it is not so favorable for practical, worldly matters; here, the imagination can do more harm than good. Trust your imagination in the creative realms, but compensate for it when making important decisions by seeking advice from someone you trust.

Harmonious

Your imaginative mind is in good rapport with your logical mind. The arts, the spiritual, and all the refined aspects of life hold interest for you. You are highly creative and have an appreciation for the subtle levels of communication between you and your partner. One of your gifts is your ability to rise above petty issues to see things from a transcendent, spiritual perspective.

Challenging

Your imagination can all too easily distort your perception, which makes it difficult to distinguish between fact and fantasy. This can cause all sorts of difficulties in communication until you compensate by constantly being willing to ask yourself, "Am I seeing things as they really are, or am I seeing things as I wish they were?" This self-questioning is critically important before making important decisions to avoid the pitfalls of Neptune's blind spot.

Mercury to Pluto

Conjunction

This aspect gives you a mental intensity that is either a great gift or a huge problem. Pluto gives your mind a passionate and even obsessive intensity that can be relentless in pursuing a mental interest. Find something healthy to feed your hungry mind, or it will turn on you, becoming obsessive over matters of no consequence. You have a "detective mind" and seem to know what is going on beneath the surface in most situations.

Harmonious

This aspect gives you the gift of mental focus. You have penetrating insights into all that you pursue mentally. Your conversations move away from the trivial and to the profound, and you are able to influence others in a favorable way; like helping a partner stay focused on moving through a difficult situation.

Challenging

Your tenacious mind latches on to issues and opinions that sometimes cause conflict. Your mind can become fixed on a point of view that you defend tenaciously, even if it is not in your best interests to do so. Until you recognize your tendency to get drawn into arguments of no consequence, these periodic intellectual power conflicts will disrupt your relationships. Learn to pick your battles wisely; ask yourself if you are really threatened before you engage in a conflict that might not be in your best interests.

Mercury to the Nodes

Conjunct the North Node

Your mind is naturally drawn to that which is growth-oriented for your soul. This is a great benefit for staying on your path of soul growth, as it is your natural mental inclination to do so.

Conjunct the South Node

You carry the past-life karma of a scholar, and intellectual pursuits come naturally to you. However, your mental development is not your path of growth, so don't spend all of your time in your mind. You can also dwell on the past, which will hold you back from growth.

Harmonious to Both Nodes

You can trust that pursuing your natural mental interests will keep you right on track for your needs for soul growth. You are able to learn from your past and apply this knowledge in your current circumstances. Communicating with others at a deep, soulful level is particularly rewarding.

Square Both Nodes

Your mind can get caught in a push-pull battle between the path of soul growth and the path of least resistance. You might know what is in your best interests to pursue, but be pulled toward that which is familiar, which then frustrates you due to its lack of meaning. You tend to get frustrated with both where you have been and where you are going. You could benefit by taming your mind, pulling it into line with that which is in your best interests. A meditation practice would be helpful.

13
Venus Through the Houses and Signs

Venus describes what turns you on, and what keeps you excited and feeling loved. Explore Venus by sign, house, and aspect to reveal your capacity to receive love, and what you would like to share with another.

Venus in Aries or the First House

You like excitement and need to keep a relationship fresh because of your constant appetite for new experiences. You value independence, both for yourself and in others, so you don't like to be held too closely in a relationship. With this placement, you could thrive in a series of short, intense, passionate relationships, but when they become routine and predictable, you move on to the next. Or, if you find someone you want to stay with, it is important for you to initiate new experiences in the relationship to keep the spark that you cherish alive.

Venus in Taurus or the Second House

You have an eye for quality in possessions and people. You don't jump into new love relationships, preferring to enjoy each cautious step toward deep love. You could be warmed to love by someone who makes you feel safe and secure, in the material world and in your relationship. Your love is long lasting and genuine, but you'll find you cannot compromise your values for love; they are that important to how you open up to others. You are affectionate and sensual in your expression of love and would thrive in a "hands-on" relationship. You are tenacious and somewhat possessive in your love interests, and prefer someone who is real and genuine as opposed to complex and mysterious.

Venus in Gemini or the Third House

The key to your heart is through your mind. Boring people need not apply for your romantic interest, as you are attracted to someone with a bright and engaging mind. Intelligence is sexy to you. You are very eclectic in your social tastes, and it would be ideal to be with a partner who gives you freedom to explore your many interests. To sustain a relationship with you, a lover would be advised to keep it interesting; you are open to almost anything except boredom and routine.

Venus in Cancer or the Fourth House

It takes you longer to warm up to love than most people because of your gentle and vulnerable emotional nature. You need to feel safe with someone before you can open to the fullness of your love, and with Cancer, you can expect to take slow, cautious steps. Once you open to love, you are the most loyal and attached of all. Venus in Cancer values family and personal life, and having someone nurture these parts of your character keeps your love strong. You enjoy private personal time together more than big group activities, and up close and personal, you are warm, loving, and affectionate.

Venus in Leo or the Fifth House

You are attracted to the dramatic and the bold in life and have a definite knack for having fun. In truth, you need to be adored to sustain your interest and you want a partner who knows how to kick up his or her heels once in awhile and have fun for the sake of fun. You like dramatic, lavish displays of love; a potential lover has to step up and offer a great deal or the royal Leo won't even notice. You want a partner you can be proud of. You like a partner who knows how to enjoy life and includes you in the celebration.

Venus in Virgo or the Sixth House

You prefer the day-to-day, shoulder-to-shoulder approach to relationships over the weekend fling. You are cautious about new love relationships, because for you to open up to love, you need to trust in the genuineness of your partner. Virgo refines Venus' normally indulgent ways, so that you feel best about yourself when you are working on yourself in some way, and practicing restraint rather than indulgence. This leads to a love of simplicity, and you prefer practical, thoughtful gifts of affection to lavish, useless, sentimental junk. Ideally, you would be with a partner who helps you overcome your feelings of inadequacy and the feeling that "I'm sure I must be doing something wrong." More than anything, you need to feel appreciated for all the little things you do to help a partner.

Venus in Libra or the Seventh House

Your refined tastes are drawn to beauty, style, and elegance. From simple to lavish, you have good taste and this will be reflected in your relationships as well. You would value a partner with style and someone who shares your interests in culture and the arts. You are a romantic and are susceptible to being charmed by the eloquent and elegant. Libra is an air sign, and you must be attracted to your partner's mind to feel sustained magnetism. You place high value on a fair, just, and honorable relationship, and will want to share important decisions with your partner. Although you would never take advantage of another, the low road leads to letting others take advantage of you for the sake of peace.

Venus in Scorpio or the Eighth House

Your passionate emotional nature must be activated for you to open to love. You crave the intimate, private aspect of the relationship, and at the same time fear for your vulnerability. Trust, trust, and more trust is what can heal you and help you sustain your feelings of love. Fear of abandonment and betrayal, jealousy, and grudges are the formidable foes you must face to open to the deepest passions of intimacy. It is simply terrible when you are with someone who activates your issues of mistrust. Even if the passion is great, mistrust can be torment, so choose wisely. You not only want to be with a partner who awakens your desire, you desire to be desired as well; it is healing to be wanted.

Venus in Sagittarius or the Ninth House

You are attracted to the adventurous type of personality—someone who you believe can expand your world. You would value a relationship that allows quite a bit of freedom; you are not looking for the joined-at-the-hip approach. You are also attracted to someone who exudes a confident, upbeat attitude about life. Traveling together would fuel the ongoing magnetism of your relationship, as would activities in nature, higher education, and philosophical and religious pursuits. You value honesty and a direct approach, and are put off by the coy and mysterious. Although physically passionate, Sagittarius is comfortable with an easygoing "pals" approach to relationships.

Venus in Capricorn or the Tenth House

You are as cautious in love as you are in most areas of life. Capricorn has a plan, and your love nature opens up when your partner fits your plan, and even more if the two of you have overlapping ambitions. Venus in Capricorn can be surprisingly romantic, but is most often put off by gushy, emotional displays of love. You prefer someone who has dignity and even self-restraint. Once given to love, you don't shake easy. Capricorn is strong on commitments and you can weather the thick and thin times of a relationship. You need to feel respected to feel loved. Capricorn, as an earth sign, is very sensual and affectionate when the mood is right, but you are most secure with the "We are building something of significance and important together" approach to sustain your love.

Venus in Aquarius or the Eleventh House

As an air sign, Aquarius is fed by the intellect, and if you are not attracted to the mental qualities of your partner, forget it. Aquarius is the most independent sign of the zodiac, and independence is something that you strongly value, both for yourself and others. The friendship level of the relationship must be authentic for your romance to be sustained—you need your lover and best friend to be the same person. You are drawn to that which makes someone stand out as unique and separate from the pack. It would be fine with you to be with a partner who wants to throw away the cultural rule book of relationships and invent it as you go along. You've never been all that attracted to fitting in with convention anyway.

Venus in Pisces or the Twelfth House

This sensitive and compassionate placement is in many ways ideal for relationships. You love romance, get totally involved in your partner's life, and can find pleasure in a wide variety of people and circumstances. In some ways, your heart is too big and gets easily hurt in relationships because of your inability to define boundaries. This starts off as being big enough to make the little sacrifices that all relationships call for; your forgiving and compassionate nature is the hallmark of your personality. But you often go too far in sacrificing your needs for your partner, which can never lead to happiness. Kindness goes a long way with you. Your romantic needs are linked to your spiritual needs and are invisible to others—only the right partner sees through the veil.

14
Venus Aspects in Your Chart

Venus aspects are particularly important to pay attention to in your chart in all matters concerning relationships. Of course, you will want to notice where your harmonious aspects suggest that it will be easy and natural for you to enjoy life, but pay particularly close attention to challenging aspects to your Venus. They challenge your ability to enjoy life and find pleasure, no matter what is actually going on in your life. Bluntly said, if your capacity to receive (Venus) is restricted, you wouldn't know it even if you had it good, *until* you learn to graciously receive compliments, offers for assistance, return favors, and the like. So if you have challenging aspects to Venus, take heart, because once you identify the restriction, you can consciously work on becoming more gracious in receiving in that area of your life, and voilà! Challenges are tests and if you pass the tests, you receive the reward of an expanded heart.

Venus to Mars

Conjunction

You have the charisma that comes from having the two cosmic lovers of the heavens, Mars and Venus, joined in your chart, creating a magnetic spark in your energy field. You are in love with love itself and must keep that spark vital in an ongoing relationship to hold your interest.

Harmonious

Your masculine and feminine energies are in harmony within you, creating ease in your relationships with others. This enhances your ability to maintain sustained, magnetic relationships.

Challenging

There is a natural tension within you between the needs of your masculine and feminine energies. You often reach for (Mars) experiences that another part of you doesn't value (Venus). This manifests as passionate and volatile relationships. Your relationships with others smooth out considerably once you recognize this tension to be an issue within you. You need to allow space for what seem to be contradictory parts of your character. Both must have room for expression in your life, and in your relationships.

Venus to Jupiter

Conjunction

This is considered one of the best aspects for luck in love. At least you will get plenty of opportunities! This shows a highly magnetic, very attractive personality. You like people and life, and people like you. Although wonderful in so many ways, you will have to watch out for an indulgent streak that is likely to manifest; too much of a good thing can be a downfall.

Harmonious

You are big-hearted and generous in relationships. You give the best and expect the best. This is the mark of the flirt, and you are skilled at playing flirtatiously with the people you interact with in the most innocent of ways.

Challenging

When these two pleasure-seeking planets are at odds in your chart, indulgences and excessiveness become an issue one way or another. There are many ways this "too-much-itis" can manifest: being too generous, expecting too much, or wanting too much, to name a few. Learning to enjoy each experience more fully before grasping for the next is the big lesson here.

Venus to Saturn

Conjunction

This aspect brings the pressure of Saturn into your love life, and can seriously restrict the flow of how much love, life, and energy you allow into your life. There are feelings of pressure, often from other people's expectations of your responsibility. To avoid being overwhelmed, you need to be discerning as to which of these responsibilities are yours, and which are not. For relationships, it has to be just right, or it is not right at all. But when you do get it right, you are strong on commitment and not likely to let it slip away.

Harmonious

You have a knack for handling the pressures and responsibilities that come with a relationship with relative ease. You don't keep making the same mistakes; you learn and integrate as you go. You are patient through the periodic trials that test any relationship.

Challenging

This aspect seriously restricts the amount of love you expect out of life. Not expecting much, you don't get much. It is almost as if you assume you are not going to get what you want, and in this willingness to compromise your values for love, your love becomes compromised at best. Learning to regain authority for your values in love can start by regaining your authority for your taste in music, color, touch, etc. This ultimately can liberate you from attracting disapproving partners into your life.

Venus to Uranus

Conjunction

You are like a square peg trying to fit into a round hole in terms of trying to conform to what your culture typically offers for relationships. You are meant to cast off cultural standards to discover your authentic self in relationships. There is likely something unusual or unique about your relationships, as your tastes are not conventional. Held too tightly, you look for escape, so you need a lot of freedom.

Harmonious

You have a way of constantly evolving in your tastes and interests, and in what is important to you in your relationships. You are able to integrate your interests into your relationships in a creative way. You are supportive of your partner's growth and independence.

Challenging

There is likely to be something unusual about your relationships; you would certainly rebel against any attempt to get you to conform to someone else's idea of who you should be. Either you attract people who have difficulties making commitments, or you are the one with this difficulty; but one way or another, you avoid commitment until you realize that you don't have to give up your independence to be in a deep relationship. The challenge is to learn how to honor the needs of a relationship, but in your own style, without sacrificing your individuality.

Venus to Neptune

Conjunction

The two levels of love, Venus (personal) and Neptune (spiritual), are merged together with this combination. You are an incurable romantic. However, you are highly susceptible to imagining qualities that aren't there in your partner, which is a set-up for disillusionment when the bubble bursts. Know this ahead of time, and ask yourself if you are falling in love with qualities that are actually present in your partner, or if you are envisioning how this person will be changed by your relationship? If it's the latter, run.

Harmonious

With the spiritual and romantic qualities of love in harmony, you have a unique ability to draw from both levels for enrichment and you have much to give because of this. You do not rely solely on your partner for love, as you know how to draw from an inner well, and this gives you more to share in your personal relationships. With your refined nature, you can experience beauty as if it were a spiritual experience. You have a healthy compassion for others, and yet their troubles don't pull you down.

Challenging

Your imagination can cause trouble in your love life with this aspect. One of the main dangers is falling in love with qualities that you only imagine to be present in your partner, but really are not. Another possibility is that you can get blindsided and taken advantage of by others, much to your surprise. Both of these potentials stem from a lack of self-worth concerning your values in love. Until you can learn to love yourself and involve yourself with what you personally find enjoyable, you'll be chasing butterflies without a net.

Venus to Pluto

Conjunction

This aspect leads to a hunger for passion at all levels of a relationship: physical, emotional, mental, and spiritual—you want it all. This can be felt as too consuming to some people, but you can't settle for casual love. You may have a push-pull battle with control issues in love. You can be highly manipulative, but then you only get what you bargained for, and the deeper levels of intimacy elude you. When you can totally surrender in love without controlling your partner, then you get the all-consuming intimacy you hunger for.

Harmonious

With the rejuvenating power of Pluto benefiting your love life, you will bounce back from wounding experiences. We all experience wounds, but you have deep healing powers to draw upon when needed. You are able to enter into trusting relationships and you skillfully avoid power games in love. This makes the deeper, transformative levels of love available for you, because you are not carrying mistrust.

Challenging

Pluto challenges bring up the dark side, and with Venus, you have likely had to face the dark side of love and sexuality one way or another. This sets up relationships to be one of your main learning arenas in this life. Fear of abandonment and betrayal, experiences of extreme jealousy and possessiveness, and confrontations with the shadow side of love . . . this is the territory of Pluto challenges with Venus. This aspect can bring a desperate quality to your most intimate relationships. It is as if you were looking for a betrayal and eventually find it. It takes deep work to access Pluto problems, and often counseling is advised to help liberate you from subconscious issues impacting your relationships. Being with someone who just loves you through your fears and desperation to bring you back to healthy, natural love would be a blessing.

Venus to Your Nodes

Conjunct Your North Node

Your values, tastes, and what you naturally find pleasurable are in natural alignment with your path for soul growth. This favorable aspect shows that what you naturally attract to you is most often in your soul's best interests as well. This links your relationship world to your path of soul growth, and when you align with your values in love, you attract a partner who is interested in soul growth as well as the pleasures of love.

Conjunct Your South Node

You seem to have an innate understanding of relationships and have much to share because of this. You have a highly magnetic nature, but you often attract opportunities for pleasure that are not in your best interests. Unless you become discerning in pleasures, you will be pulled away from your growth by indulgences. You may also attract many people into your life with whom you sense a deep familiarity, as in past-life connections. Again, unless you are discerning as to whether these relationships are supportive to what you are building in this life, you can become seduced off your path.

Harmonious to Both Nodes

You have refined your values so that they are naturally supportive of your path of soul growth. You attract people and situations to you that are in your best interests. Even your social life can be supportive of your path of growth. You bring out this quality of soul growth in your most personal relationships and for you, spiritual life is rooted in love, beauty, and the arts.

Square Both Nodes

You are not likely to find much pleasure in what the culture around you offers for soul growth or relationships. This dissatisfaction exists until you break free of the cultural attitudes in both regards and discover what is personally meaningful for you in terms of soul growth and relationships. Until then, you will attract people and situations that do not support your path of growth.

15
Mars Through the Houses and Signs

Mars indicates how you initiate action, express your passion, and express your anger, and is vitally important in your relationships. After all, it is the supporting male actor in the play of your life, how you go about asserting yourself, act on your will, defend yourself with anger when necessary, and express yourself through passion. Whether you are a man or a woman, all of this will have a direct bearing on your relationships. If blocked, you become ineffectual in acting on your best behalf. If overexpressed, other people will perceive you as being hostile. Yet, if integrated into your personality, you find healthy expression for your passions, and become effective at initiating activities and skillful at defending yourself when the need arises.

The sign that your Mars is in describes the most natural way for you to align with your power. The house Mars is in describes where in your life you will be tested with this power.

Mars in Aries or the First House

Initiating Action

Mars is the ruler of Aries and is at its strongest in this sign, giving you an incredible ability to get things going. The planet of action in the sign of action translates as action, your second name. You need a relationship that gives you plenty of freedom to do what you want, when you want. More than likely, the relationship activities will center on your interests; but then, you are the one who initiates things.

Expressing Anger

When you are hemmed in and feel blocked in your actions by the expectations of others, trouble erupts. In conflict, no one's energy can rise faster than yours, and you prove equal to any challenge, almost enjoying the sport. One of the attributes of your quick temper is that once you express your anger, it doesn't linger.

In Passion

You act on your considerable passion in the spontaneous moment, and it is probably true that you enjoy the chase. Routines bore you; thus passion is always connected to exploring something new and exciting.

Mars in Taurus or the Second House

Initiating Action

You apply your energy with a great deal of determination, an eye for quality, and drive for completion. The low road would lead to others experiencing you as too headstrong, stubborn, and inflexible. You do know how to get what you want, but be willing to ask yourself, "At what cost?"

Expressing Anger

You will never back down to intimidation or pushy behavior. Your great strength is your ability to hold your ground in conflict. Your anger is a slow boil, but when pushed, "mad as a bull" describes your temper.

In Passion

You have a highly developed sense of touch, adding sensuality to your sexuality. Your passion rises slowly, as you prefer to take your time and linger in each pleasurable moment.

Mars in Gemini or the Third House

Initiating Action

You do not generally move in a straight line; the Twins of Gemini will pull you into various activities on the way to getting something else done. You are at your energetic best when you are doing a few different things at once. This drives everyone else crazy, but it is when you feel the best.

Expressing Anger

You are skilled at avoiding arguments and equally skilled at talking yourself in and out of trouble. You can use your cleverness as an avoidance technique, making you very hard to pin down in an argument, but when you do blow, your command of language can unleash a verbal onslaught.

In Passion

The intellect is an important doorway to your sexuality, and your curiosity has to be aroused to awaken the passion of Mars. You need some variety in your lovemaking styles to sustain your interest.

Mars in Cancer or the Fourth House

Initiating Action

You have to feel emotionally involved to bring out the natural power of your Mars. You are at your best when you are operating within defined boundaries within which you already feel safe. You are slow to let others into your innermost circle, but once you accept someone into your trust, you are the most loyal of all. You need outlets for your nurturing energy, and enjoy shared activities related to the home, house, family, and land within a relationship. You initiate action in cautious and caring ways.

Expressing Anger

Your anger is expressed with emotional intensity and only shown to those you feel safest with; strangely, this leads to you only striking out at those you love. The paradox continues in that you express your emotional sensitivity (Cancer) with anger and intensity (Mars). You are extremely protective and willing to go to battle for those you love.

In Passion

Your passion is awakened only with the deepest of emotional bonds; engaging in casual sex wouldn't even cross your mind. Your sexual energy can be experienced as nurturing for both you and your partner.

Mars in Leo or the Fifth House

Initiating Action

You initiate activity with great gusto, dramatic flair, and a show of confidence, whether you feel it or not. This is a "work hard, play hard" combination, as you want to live life to the fullest.

Expressing Anger

Mars in the fire sign of Leo shows that you can be fierce in your expression of anger; no one can overwhelm you in power conflicts. You can always win, but this is not always in your best interests, as it would create a very shallow learning curve in life. You need to be willing to examine where your pride is getting in the way of cooperative involvements.

In Passion

In romance, Mars in Leo is a star. You pour your heart and soul into your passion. This is a healthy outlet for the Leo pride, unless you focus too much on performance sex, thereby missing the intimate connection. A heartfelt connection brings joy and playfulness into your passion.

Mars in Virgo or the Sixth House

Initiating Action

You set about your activities with a plan. You like to think things through to minimize mistakes, and then do what you do impeccably. You apply yourself with the eye of the perfectionist. Although this is a fine standard to set for yourself, when you turn your critical eye toward your partner's behavior, trouble erupts. You do like to help out in your friends' and partner's lives. Your health and fitness is important to you and is a fine place to apply your exacting standards.

Expressing Anger

Your intellect is as sharp as a tack and when provoked, you can cut your opponent to shreds. You likely express more frustration than anger, and when you get in a critical mood, you can find fault everywhere.

In Passion

You have discriminating taste when it comes to passion, particularly with health and hygiene. You have to curb the tendency to be so busy that there is no time for romance, though Virgo is naturally sensual and technically skilled as a lover.

Mars in Libra or the Seventh House

Initiating Action

You initiate action after much deliberation, sometimes too much. You are highly cooperative and a natural for the give and take of relationships. You would rather cooperate than coerce, and are not comfortable around belligerent or intimidating personalities; you are a natural team player.

Expressing Anger

You have a natural refinement in the expression of your warrior energy, and anger is not typically safe territory for you, so you become skilled at dodging issues rather than confronting them directly. Your power is in your diplomacy and your ability to negotiate honorable agreements with others. You are disempowered when you accommodate other people's needs at the expense of your own to avoid conflict.

In Passion

Your passionate nature is refined in Libra, showing that it is unnatural for you to throw yourself with complete abandon into your passions; you like to maintain a degree of balance. The courtship and style of a relationship are important aspects of romance for you—style counts.

Mars in Scorpio or the Eighth House

Initiating Action

You are cautious, controlled, and calculating in the way you initiate action. You are shrewd and have a somewhat skeptical perspective on all issues concerning trust. You could be skilled in investment strategies, research, and psychology, and, of course, the bedroom. If you get hooked by the low road of mistrust and never forget a wound, you will be held to your past and won't be able to initiate anything.

Expressing Anger

With Scorpio, still waters run deep, and this describes your psychological-warfare approach to anger. Resentment leading to plans for retaliation can be a big hook for you, and if you can't examine your own behavior, this can lead to a "Never forgive, never forget" attitude. If you have the character strength to examine the hidden side of your own character that is revealed in difficulties, this is deeply transformative in and of itself; then you can avoid all the armor building, and keep your heart open.

In Passion

This is your theater; passion be thy name! Mars is very strong in Scorpio and adds a psychological component to your intimacy. Ideally, you would be with a partner with an equal appetite in this regard, because intimacy can be close to magical with the right partner. Trust issues will come up. A fear of abandonment and betrayal haunts everyone with Scorpio, and all of the beauty of this placement turns dark when mistrust issues arise, so choose wisely.

Mars in Sagittarius or the Ninth House

Initiating Action

You move forward in life with optimism and enthusiasm and thrive on momentum. You need a bit of space to feel your best, and outdoor activities and travel will always capture your interest. This expansive quality may also be found pursuing higher education, politics, religion, and the world of the higher mind.

Expressing Anger

You may seem casual and happy-go-lucky, but Sagittarius is a fire sign and those arrows can be weapons; thus you can become quite fierce in anger situations. You can become quite high-minded and scorch your opponent with moralistic tirades when provoked.

In Passion

You are an ardent and enthusiastic lover. Sagittarius tends toward indulgent behavior, and this placement is known for being readily given to pursuing its passions. Your passions are awakened by a bit of playfulness from your partner.

Mars in Capricorn or the Tenth House

Initiating Action

You are a master planner and organizer and are most effective when you are in absolute control of your time. Tenacious and persevering, you get involved in that which pays off through time. In relationships, you also control the initiation and organization of activities.

Expressing Anger

Capricorn's strategy in battle is to assume the role of the ultimate authority, and you maintain your position of power by maintaining your control. There are times when control might even be inhibition, but even then it looks like strength to others. When coming from this place of absolute authority, your anger can be crushing to another in its calculated strike. Issues around accountability and punctuality can be hot spots for your demanding standards.

In Passion

You need deep commitment to be at your best with passion, and then intimacy can be one of the great releases from your normal task-oriented approach to life. Capricorn is highly appreciative of the sensuality of the experience and enjoys sustained foreplay.

Mars in Aquarius or the Eleventh House

Initiating Action

Your highly independent nature is at its best when uninhibited by other people's expectations; thus you require a relationship that allows considerable freedom. You are not interested at all in doing things in any sort of conventional way and will even go out of your way not to be conventional. You have to be your own person.

Expressing Anger

Aquarius is not timid in anger, and if you feel your principles are at stake, watch out. Aquarius is the rebel, the revolutionary, or the reformer. At the rebel stage, you can strike out just for the right to strike out. At the revolutionary level, you've got a cause that is larger than yourself to focus your anger on. And at the reformer level, you drop the anger, roll up your sleeves, and dedicate yourself proactively to a cause you believe in.

In Passion

As an air sign, Aquarius needs intellectual stimulation to sustain passionate interest in another. Friendship will be equally important; your lover has to be your best friend. Given this, Mars in Aquarius will be very liberated and uninhibited in exploring the frontiers of passion.

Mars in Pisces or the Twelfth House

Initiating Action

Pisces, the sign of the Fishes, is responsive to the tugs and pulls of the emotional watery realm. Mars can feel muddled in Pisces as far as knowing what action to take. This leads to circuitous, indirect ways of asserting yourself. Because of this, you might find that you do well with a partner who enjoys taking the initiative.

Expressing Anger

Anger is not your strong suit. Mars tends to implode with the confusion caused by anger. You can feel guilty if you hurt another, so you tend to internalize the anger, making it very difficult for your partner to know what your issues are. You typically won't express your anger in the moment, but, for the sake of keeping the air clear in your relationships, you can learn to educate your partner, after the fact, as to what pushed your buttons.

In Passion

This can be one of your strengths in relationships, as this placement leads to a bit of the incurable romantic with a sensitive and imaginative approach to lovemaking. Pisces likes to please, and you will experience as much pleasure from your partner's pleasure as you do from your own, making you a very attentive and romantic partner.

16
Mars Aspects in Your Chart

Mars to Jupiter

Conjunction

This aspect greatly expands your energy field, and with your positive outlook, you like to take on a great many activities. You assert yourself in a strong yet positive way, allowing you to avoid considerable conflict. You create a life that has abundance of passion and activity, all of it born from your positive will. You will have to watch a strong tendency toward excessive behavior of all sorts with this combination. You can easily overwhelm others if you don't find healthy outlets for your abundant energy.

Harmonious

You are an enthusiast in all that you do and have the ability to be assertive without being insensitive and to define your boundaries without being rude. You have a natural ability to move away from defensive reactions and become proactive in choosing what to direct your energy toward.

Challenging

This aspect often leads to inappropriate choices of action on your part. This could manifest as a highly defensive temperament if unrestrained. This combination could lead to impatience, excessive grasping, and competitiveness, particularly in philosophical, religious, and political issues. Basically, the male, aggressive, warrior energy of Mars is out of control until you are able to identify this inappropriate excessiveness and demonstrate restraint with its impulses.

Mars to Saturn

Conjunction

Either you have developed tremendous self-discipline, or you feel frustrated and blocked in your expression of your energy—it is one way or the other with the demanding pressure of Saturn sitting on your Mars shoulder of action. With self-control, you can achieve anything; without it, the deck seems stacked against you. To you, commitments are binding—if you say you are going to do something, you feel bound to that until it is completed. Furthermore, you demand this same accountability from others.

Harmonious

You are highly effective in all that you set out to accomplish. You have a disciplined, patient, and persevering will that gives you a steadiness in handling responsibilities, which you carry out with relative grace. You are able to be direct without being stern, and this keeps the air clear in relationships. You rarely make the same mistake twice, and you've got staying power.

Challenging

Your will for action runs up against the disapproval of authority. This is acutely frustrating, and because it has never been easy to gain approval, a lack confidence results. It is too easy for you to feel rejected before you even try, until you internalize your relationship to authority. As long as it is external (needing approval from others), you are vulnerable to their disapproval, effectively freezing action before it begins. By passing the test and demonstrating the self-control that comes from being your own authority, much of the pressure that you feel from others dissipates. You are still cautious, but not inhibited.

Mars to Uranus

Conjunction

Uranus demands that you cast off all external expectations and do things your own way. This gives you an independent streak a mile and a half wide that, if not handled wisely, can cause as much trouble as good. The low road is the rebel, always having just cause for being fired up and angry. Repressing anger doesn't work either; it will burst forth in unpredictable moments. The high road comes from shifting from fighting for your right to be free, and instead, getting on to expressing this inherent gift by having the courage to follow a path that is authentically you.

Harmonious

You have a gift for being innovative in the ways you assert yourself—you never get stuck. You always see a new way to deal with a situation, and this allows you to maneuver skillfully past petty power struggles and annoyances. You are also highly persuasive and encourage others to be more independent in their lives. You help a relationship stay vital by pursuing new paths of discovery in your own life and bringing what you learn into the relationship.

Challenging

Your need for independence often stands in the way of relationships. You rebel at any attempt by your partner to control, restrict, or even direct your energy. Your need to do things your own way is experienced as uncooperative by others, but you detest falling in line just because everyone else does. You have particular difficulty with stupid rules and stupid people. It bugs you to no end when others interfere with what you want to do. This can lead to a hair-trigger defensive reaction to any challenge (or perceived challenge). Until you can get a handle on this, it will likely be disruptive in relationships. Eastern martial arts training, as a metaphor or literally, would give you the skills to pull back to your center before reacting to anger or impulse.

Mars to Neptune

Conjunction

This aspect brings the dreamy, imaginative, romantic qualities of Neptune to the male, aggressive, warrior part of your character. You are meant to be more a lover than a fighter. The artistic and mystical aspects of life are favored, and this can certainly make you an imaginative and sensitive lover. This also is known as a blind-spot aspect, so you are advised to analyze your motivations, and the worst-case and best-case scenarios of your plans, before you make important decisions.

Harmonious

This aspect can lead to inspired activity, and definitely softens the edge of Mars' normally aggressive ways. This gives a natural ability to rise above petty concerns and direct your energy in more creative ways. You can bring the imaginative and even spiritual qualities of Neptune into how you pursue your passions, but are probably too subtle in the expression of your anger for the other person to clearly get it.

Challenging

Your imagination often causes problems in distorting your motivations for action. When you think back to some of the poorer choices you've likely made, you first wonder, "What was I thinking?" But upon examination, you weren't thinking, you were *imagining* potential that didn't exist, or you were choosing not to pay attention to the clues of someone who was taking advantage of you. You are vulnerable in these ways and are advised to compensate for this before acting. Ask yourself if you have seen the full-case scenario before you choose to act. This can help you avoid acting from Neptune's blind spot.

Mars to Pluto

Conjunction

This aspect leads to a type of superpower being expressed through your will. Your power comes off much stronger than you ever expect or intend. The sheer force of your personality intimidates many who feel threatened in your presence, and there are certain to be many power conflicts to deal with. Yours is the test of the right use of this power. A little bit of passion activates a tremendous amount of passion, as if you were connecting with the collective archetypal level of passion. There are some places in a relationship where this is of course delightful, but watch out for passionate anger; you feel as if you could annihilate your adversary, and you could, but is it in your best interests to do so?

You need to have healthy outlets for this passionate part of your character at all times, or it will erupt in power conflicts.

Mars to the Nodes

Conjunct Your North Node

Your path of courage is the same as your path of soul growth. Your path of soul growth requires you to express your Mars in a healthy way by standing up for what is important and having the courage to act on your plans.

Conjunct Your South Node

You have a tendency to submit to the path of least resistance. Some of this may truly be a Taoist going with the flow, but much of it is likely indulging yourself rather than developing any self-control. You come into this life with an inherent understanding of the male psyche, but it is not easy to move forward in life with the attitude of "Why make things difficult—why not just take it easy?" Some talents undoubtedly do come to you effortlessly, as if you inherited them from your past lives.

Harmonious to Both Nodes

Your choice of actions tends to keep you on your path of soul growth. You readily align your will with that which is in your best interests and motivate others to take the high road in their lives as well.

Square Both Nodes

You often sabotage your path by asserting yourself in ways that neither take advantage of your natural abilities nor lead to any real growth. You then tend to get angry over things not going your way. You particularly need to examine your motivations before acting with these questions in mind: "Am I choosing a course of action that takes advantage of my natural abilities? Am I choosing a course of action that is truly growth-oriented for me?"

17
Jupiter Through the Houses and Signs

Jupiter describes your style of generosity and relationship goals.

Jupiter in Aries or the First House

Style of Generosity

You give of yourself and interject inspirational, enthusiastic support for your partner. You are naturally motivational.

Relationship Goals

A relationship that maintains a quality of freshness, newness, even a bit of a pioneering approach to life, would be rewarding to you. You will also thrive in a relationship that gives plenty of room for independent action.

Jupiter in Taurus or the Second House

Style of Generosity

You are the connoisseur of gift giving, taking pride in choosing gifts that reflect the values of the person you are gifting. You are generous with money as well, but need to be careful not to give beyond your means.

Relationship Goals

You can enjoy dreaming with your partner of ways to enhance and improve your material world. For non-shoppers, involvement with nature can be a rewarding relationship activity.

Jupiter in Gemini or the Third House

Style of Generosity

You value learning and staying informed, and like to give books, magazine subscriptions, tickets to events, etc., as gifts. You also enjoy helping people become aware of the options that are available, from entertainment to professional.

Relationship Goals

Your goals with Jupiter in the sign of the Twins are wide open and eclectic. You are curious about almost everything, and won't let your relationships ever get boring. You would thrive in a relationship with great communication.

Jupiter in Cancer or the Fourth House

Style of Generosity

You have a personal touch in your generosity, often giving gifts that have a nostalgic meaning to you and the person you are gifting. You like to make a big deal of birthdays and anniversaries and other personal meaningful days. Cooking a special meal for someone, or arranging special dinners out, are also natural ways of giving for Jupiter in Cancer.

Relationship Goals

You are looking for your personal life to be rewarding and enriching. Cancer relates to home, house, and family, and some variation of this theme will likely be part of your relationship goals.

Jupiter in Leo or the Fifth House

Style of Generosity

"Life is grand, come and enjoy it with me" captures your attitude of generosity. Treating people to entertainment events or throwing lavish parties can also fit your temperament.

Relationship Goals

Jupiter in Leo wants to keep the spark of romance, courtship, and fun alive in the relationship. Big plans, big goals, grand vacations . . . ah, the celebratory life is all you want.

Jupiter in Virgo or the Sixth House

Style of Generosity

The Virgo sense of practicality influences the nature of your generosity, and you give gifts that people can use. You like to give of your time and want to pitch in and help your friends and partners as a way of being generous.

Relationship Goals

Simplicity is the way for Virgo, and your goals will reflect this. A healthy and manageable lifestyle with a partner who wants to pitch in and make it happen is what you might have as a relationship goal.

Jupiter in Libra or the Seventh House

Style of Generosity

Libra has very refined taste, and your generosity will reflect this. Taking your partner out for an elegant and cultural evening is a favorite, and with your taste, gifts of clothes, jewelry, books, and tickets to cultural events would be natural.

Relationship Goals

Libra is interested in the relationship itself, not just the other person, and the goal of a harmonious relationship comes with the territory. Beautifying the home and garden and sharing cultural interests together are examples of relationship goals.

Jupiter in Scorpio or the Eighth House

Style of Generosity

While some people like making a public display of their generosity, you prefer not to. You would rather wait for a private moment, and like to give a gift that only you and your sweetheart understand the meaning of.

Relationship Goals

Goals related to shared investments and other financial pursuits would be natural for you. Research projects together could also be rewarding, but most important of all, an intimate relationship is what you are seeking.

Jupiter in Sagittarius or the Ninth House

Style of Generosity

Jupiter in Sagittarius knows no boundaries, and this describes your generosity. You like to go over the top and give more than is expected of you. Never underestimate the value of your positive attitude on life. Your generosity can also take the form of encouragement for others in their lives.

Relationship Goals

You look at life as an expansive field of opportunities, and your goals in relationship are to explore life together as travelers, scholars, or spiritual seekers. Big goals and big dreams are your style, and you want a partner with whom you can dream up new adventures together.

Jupiter in Capricorn or the Tenth House

Style of Generosity

Capricorn is a pragmatic sign, and this describes the nature of your generosity. You like to give gifts that have practical value and shy away from the ostentatious. In truth, gift giving is not your natural style; you would rather help someone with a project or provide guidance as a way of being generous.

Relationship Goals

You are a builder, and you will value a relationship that has the long-term goal of constantly improving your standard of living together by working hard on shared ambitions.

Jupiter in Aquarius or the Eleventh House

Style of Generosity

You like to give gifts that reflect your love of the uniqueness in life. You like to give gifts when they are not expected, but you likely experience resistance to obligatory gift giving.

Relationship Goals

The goal of a quality friendship within your relationships is natural for this placement. Unique vacations, shared involvement with important social causes, and for some, joining groups with like-minded souls would be rewarding.

Jupiter in Pisces or the Twelfth House

Style of Generosity

You like giving gifts that have sentimental value. Making the personal sacrifice of forsaking something for yourself in order to give to another feels especially rewarding.

Relationship Goals

With your active imagination, you will certainly want to keep the romance alive in the relationship. With your compassionate nature, you would value a relationship with shared goals of helping those in need.

18
Jupiter Aspects in Your Chart

Jupiter to Saturn

Conjunction

You have a knack for instinctively aligning with professional and social goals that your culture rewards. You periodically go through a birthing of new career interests.

Harmonious

You are patient in achieving your goals and have a natural ability to expand your career and social ambitions in measured steps.

Challenging

You lack confidence in reaching for your goals and need to battle through a fear of failure to achieve your potential. You need a relationship that builds your confidence, but tend to attract partners who disapprove of your goals.

Jupiter to Uranus

Conjunction

This aspect leads to excitement about discovering the opportunities the future holds and very little sentimental attachment to how things were in the past. You have the gift of being innovative in your forward movement, but probably need to cultivate the ability to enjoy your here-and-now reality, or your great reward will always remain just around the corner.

Harmonious

You have a "can do" attitude that leads to what appears to others as a lucky life. You never get stuck when obstacles present themselves on the way to your goals, because you take the challenge on as a sport, remaining enthusiastic as you tirelessly try new options until you succeed.

Challenging

You are often impatient with reaching your goals, which can lead to rash and, at worst, reckless behavior. You hold the image of the rebel dear to your philosophical outlook on life. This rebellious attitude, combined with your irrepressible urge for freedom, can be stumbling blocks to carrying on a relationship. By finding social causes that could benefit from your paradigm-busting attitude, you take the heat off your relationships as being the outlet for your rebellion.

Jupiter to Neptune

Conjunction

With the two most idealistic planets together in your chart, you are able to put a positive spin on most everything. There are times when you are inspired as if touched by a vision. There are other times when your positive spin is really denial and avoidance in disguise. Until you realize that illusion often comes masked as inspiration, this visionary gift of yours causes as much trouble as good. Try to imagine your plans in full-case scenario before you act, to avoid Neptune's blind spot.

Harmonious

You are guided by a powerful faith that silently sustains you in all your endeavors. You are led to appropriate goals and you know when you are on track when you can see your goals through to completion in your mind's eye.

Challenging

Jupiter expands the misuse of your imagination with a challenging aspect to Neptune. Unrealistic optimism? Excessive fear? Until you gain some discipline with your imagination, you will be susceptible to fantasy masquerading as fact and the inevitable poor choices that come from not seeing things as they really are.

Jupiter to Pluto

Conjunction

This aspect will fuel your drive to experience the fullness of life with Pluto's high-octane passion. There is the danger of blind ambition or even ruthlessness if this driven energy is not tempered with an ethical code to guide your conduct. Pluto gives depth to Jupiter's expansive philosophy, leading to a desire to understand the mysteries of life and death.

Harmonious

You have the ability to draw on deep reserves of energy in the pursuit of your goals. This is because you are not prone to set superficial goals, and instead focus on that which has deep meaning to you. This gives you natural leadership ability, which you are able to handle with relative grace.

Challenging

Pluto distorts the goals of Jupiter when these two planets are in challenging aspect. This combination can describe an excessive hunger for power, leading to a life philosophy that "the ends justify the means." This attitude of reaching for the fullness of what is available is not problematic in and of itself, and it certainly prevents settling for mediocrity. The problem comes when blind ambition becomes ruthless in its impact on others. You can minimize this concern by reviewing your motivations, and the consequences of your plans on others, before you act.

Jupiter to the Nodes

Conjunct Your North Node

Your goals are naturally linked to your path of soul growth. This gives very little attachment to your past as you all too willingly move toward your future.

Conjunct Your South Node

The expansive qualities of Jupiter are part of your heritage from your past lives. This can lead to feelings of entitlement and a nostalgic yearning for the "good old days."

Harmonious to Both Nodes

Your positive attitude allows you to learn from your past and apply what you have learned to your path of soul growth.

Square Both Nodes

You are working through the karma of excessiveness in this life. You get overly confident about your ability to dabble in the indulgences of your past without getting sidetracked from your path of soul growth.

19
Saturn Through the Houses and Signs

Saturn describes how you are being tested, and the nature of your challenges on your way to self-mastery. Because of the difficult nature of Saturn in our individual lives, Saturn will prove to be a testing area in your relationships as well. The difficulty of Saturn is that it demands something of you: self-mastery. This is a tall order, and when you resist this pressure, you experience it outside of yourself, specifically through your relationships. This process is called "projection": when you deny a quality in yourself, you will attract its expression to you from others, typically in its worst-case scenario. That which we can't see in ourselves, we project on to others so we can experience the energy vicariously, as if it were happening to us, rather than being part of us.

Saturn is the slow and steady path of overcoming your fears, insecurities, and shortcomings on the way to becoming your own authority in life. In youth, authority is appropriately external through parents, school, and the protocol of the culture. To fully engage Saturn is to become your own authority in the sign and house it occupies in your chart. But it is never easy. Here is precisely where you will have fears and insecurities.

Thus it takes continuous self-control, self-restraint, and self-discipline to achieve the self-mastery Saturn demands.

On the way to developing self-mastery, Saturn appears as the very qualities you most dislike in others (projection). Pay attention to what you most dislike about your partner and see if this is somehow connected to your own Saturn!

Saturn in Aries or the First House

Test
The test here is to learn the right restraint of the Aries impulse to action—when to act and when not to act.

Projected
Mild: With a fear of acting on your own impulse, you have a dislike for assertive individuals, feeling they have no sensitivity for others. *Strong:* You attract domineering types of partners who always know what they want to do, and you get pulled into their activities, while your inspirations remain on the back burner.

Integrated
You know how to stand up for what is important to you and can initiate activities of your choice. However, when situations don't require you to assert yourself, or your partner needs you to listen, you are able to patiently restrain your will.

Saturn in Taurus or the Second House

Test
The test here is knowing that your skills, talents, and abilities are plenty adequate to provide for yourself—security through self-reliance. Another test is knowing how to enjoy the material world without getting caught in its traps.

Projected
Mild: With a fear of the inability to create abundance in your own life, you have a dislike for wealthy people who demonstrate their wealth through their possessions. *Strong:* With a strong fear of the inability to provide financial security for yourself, you attract relationships with people who provide for you financially, but are overly focused on their possessions as their only measure of happiness.

Integrated

You have learned how to enjoy the material world and its bounty without becoming attached to your possessions as your only measure of security. You've learned that living a life of integrity that is aligned with your values is worth more than money.

Saturn in Gemini or the Third House

Test

The test here is to overcome feelings of intellectual inferiority and to stay open-minded, communicative, and informed.

Projected

Mild: With a fear of inadequacy in communicating, you dislike talkers and those who dominate conversations. *Strong:* Fearing your own intellectual inferiority, you attract know-it-all partners who dominate every conversation.

Integrated

You have disciplined your mind to stay open-minded and to be just as skilled at listening as you are at speaking. You honor your responsibility to be informed by constantly educating yourself one way or another.

Saturn in Cancer or the Fourth House

Test

The test here is to overcome your fear of not being able to provide emotional support for others. Another test is to learn to nurture without suffocating your partner.

Projected

Mild: Fearing you will get swallowed up in your own emotions, you dislike people who give in to their emotions, judging them as being weak. *Strong:* With a fear of dealing with your own emotions, you tend to attract either those who are totally emotional about everything, or those who can't get in touch with their emotions at all.

Integrated

You have learned to take responsibility for your own emotional well-being by providing nurturing situations for yourself. You know how to define your boundaries, allowing you to feel safe in taking on responsibilities for emotionally caring for those in your circle of trust.

Saturn in Leo or the Fifth House

Test

The test here is to face the question "Is it the power of love or the love of power that most guides your life?" Another test is to overcome the fear of expression and to develop a strong ego, yet keep it in proper restraint so as to not become prideful.

Projected

Mild: With a fear of projecting your own personality, you dislike strong, flamboyant personalities. *Strong:* With an inability to stand up for your own ego needs, you attract partners with domineering personalities and huge egos.

Integrated

You have learned how to take pride in what you have done well, but not let pride get in the way of your personal relationships. You have a strong ego and personality, yet they are under control so as to not dominate every situation.

Saturn in Virgo or the Sixth House

Test

The test here is to overcome insecurity and a fear of failure. Another test is to overcome excessive critical self-analysis by developing proactive disciplines for self-improvement.

Projected

Mild: With an inability to get your own life together, you have a dislike for perfectionists and detail-minded people. You think of them as small-minded. *Strong:* With a fear of facing your own inner critic, you attract partners who have a critical outlook on most everything.

Integrated

You have learned to learn from your mistakes, rather than fear them. You keep yourself humble and have integrated a discipline of self-improvement into your life.

Saturn in Libra or the Seventh House

Test

The test here is to overcome the fear of not being able to stand up for what is fair by becoming a skilled and fair negotiator, bringing out honor and integrity in all of your agreements.

Projected

Mild: With a fear of not being liked by others, you have a negative reaction to people who are too polite or nice. You suspect them of being insincere. *Strong:* With your fear of having to deal with people who are unfair or unjust, you attract this very quality in others, forcing you to constantly compromise your values to placate others to avoid conflict.

Integrated

You have learned how to negotiate fair, just, and honorable agreements in all your relationships. You have gone beyond the passive role of simply wishing for fairness in life, and have learned how to be clever enough, diligent enough, and patient enough to settle for nothing less than that which is in everyone's best interests.

Saturn in Scorpio or the Eighth House

Test

The test here is to overcome mistrust. The low road of "Never forgive, never forget" has to be overcome, or mistrust will control your life.

Projected

Mild: With insecurities about your own sexuality, you dislike people who act or dress in sexy ways. *Strong:* With mistrust and a fear of facing the issues from your past, you attract unforgiving partners who keep their deeper emotions guarded and hidden.

Integrated

When problems erupt in your relationships, you have developed the character strength to look into the hidden side of your own psyche for clues of what you need to work on within yourself to improve the situation. This frees you from the blame game and allows you to keep your heart open to intimacy.

Saturn in Sagittarius or the Ninth House

Test

The test here is overcoming biases, prejudices, and dogmatic philosophical/religious views on life to become an open-minded and disciplined seeker/student/teacher.

Projected

Mild: With an inability to claim your own truth, you have an adverse reaction to those who proselytize their religious and political views. *Strong:* With an inability to examine your own beliefs, you attract partners who moralize and proselytize their views on life without any ability to self-examine.

Integrated

You seek out relationships based on honesty and a respect for each other's lofty principles. You have learned that there are many truths on the way to understanding the one truth. You are a natural teacher of philosophical issues because of your understanding of abstract issues and your ability to bring them down to earth for others.

Saturn in Capricorn or the Tenth House

Test

The first test here is overcoming the fear of failure, and later, overcoming the tendency to look at everything in terms of how it aligns with your career ambitions.

Projected

Mild: With a fear of failure, you having a strong dislike for those who focus on achievement as their measure of success in life. *Strong:* An inability to act on your ambitions can lead to attracting partners who are all work and no play; partners who are strong on commitment and following the rules, but short on fun and romance.

Integrated

You have learned how to take absolute responsibility for your life and are successful without sacrificing your personal life. You have not limited the drive for self-mastery exclusively to your professional life, and have acquired the discipline that it takes to have a full life. In relationships, you have found a partner with shared ambitions and you enjoy building a life together.

Saturn in Aquarius or the Eleventh House

Test

The test here is becoming responsible for your independence and individuality so that you are not fighting for the right to be free, but expressing it in a responsible way. Another test is becoming detached enough from a situation to see the big picture, but not so detached as to be insensitive to the needs of others.

Projected

Mild: With a fear of seeming different from others, you have a dislike for those who are highly individualistic in their lifestyle. *Strong:* With an inability to claim your own independence, you attract partners who are so independent that they cannot make any commitments whatsoever.

Integrated

Aquarius is where the "I" becomes part of a "We." You have found a responsible way to contribute to the collective well-being, while doing this in a way that honors your uniqueness and individuality. In relationships, you have learned that it takes unconditional acceptance of the uniqueness of others to integrate friendship into your important relationships.

Saturn in Pisces or the Twelfth House

Test

The test here is overcoming the tendency toward martyrdom, self-sacrifice, and self-denial by developing a disciplined spiritual life that is empowering for your self-esteem.

Projected

Mild: With a fear of your emotions, you dislike sentimentality and people who express their emotional sensitivities. *Strong:* A stronger projection of this placement is attracting relationships with victim-type partners who are never able to stand up for themselves; it is only your support of them that keeps them going.

Integrated

You have learned to take responsibility for your emotional boundaries and will not be guilted or shamed into activity. Instead, you have learned how to responsibly act on your compassion by finding healthy ways of serving others, without sacrificing yourself.

20
Saturn Aspects in Your Chart

Saturn to Uranus

Conjunction

You have a gift for being innovative in the way you fulfill responsibilities. You need to have the freedom for self-direction in your career and other areas of responsibility, or the rebellious side of your character will cause problems. With self-direction, you have a knack for changing with the times, and periodically you totally revamp your life.

Harmonious

You are able to express your individuality in the ways you fulfill your responsibilities. You don't get frustrated easily, because you are always innovative when challenges present themselves. You readily adapt to the changing conditions of the world.

Challenging

You often get frustrated when your responsibilities conflict with your need for independence and freedom, and then you resist change when change is necessary. You have to come to philosophical terms with this conflict; otherwise, you are set up to resist the very responsibilities you sign up for with your independent choices. It has been said that freedom comes from joyfully fulfilling responsibilities, and this is an apt lesson for you to learn.

Saturn to Neptune

Conjunction

The high road of this aspect leads to the ability to provide form and structure for your creative and spiritual inclinations. The low road is when your fears, illusions, and escapist tendencies undermine your ability to be effective in the world. The path is clear: discipline (Saturn) must be linked to imagination (Neptune) in a proactive way, as in creative visualization and meditation, or you become vulnerable to the illusionary side of Neptune.

Harmonious

You don't let the pressures of the world bog you down. When life is challenging, you have the ability to set an issue aside, rise above the situation and see it from a bigger perspective, and then apply these creative insights into resolving the conflict in front of you.

Challenging

This aspect leads to periodic bouts of doubt, insecurity, and even fear concerning your ability to handle the pressures of your life. This is a test of faith, because your ability to handle responsibility is undermined by your imagination. Your challenge is to learn that fear and faith are flip sides of the same coin; if you are experiencing fear, you are not practicing the discipline of faith. Getting a handle on this discipline makes all the difference in the world.

Saturn to Pluto

Conjunction

You can become a powerful authority, as this aspect fuels ambition and gives you natural authoritative influence over others. How will you use this? Will you deny it, encountering negative, authoritative power? Will you misuse this manipulative power that you have been given for your personal gain? Or will you use it in a way that benefits yourself and others? The high road gives you the ability to coalesce a group's point of view with that which is in everyone's best interests.

Harmonious

You have a natural ability to handle responsibility and administrative positions of authority. You bend, but do not break. You can go through setbacks and delays, but never defeat, as you draw upon deep reserves of soul power to see you through. You can be very influential on many levels in life because others defer to your authority, which you are able to handle with relative grace—as if it were the most natural thing in the world for you to do.

Challenging

There will no doubt be various times in your life when you get drawn into huge power conflicts, and even times when you have to confront the shadow side of yourself and others. Left unchecked, this could undermine your attempts to maintain well-being, as you would always be on guard for a perceived threat. You have seen the misuse of power and rightfully believe that power corrupts, but this attitude keeps you at odds with your own success. A proactive way of engaging this combination is to commit yourself to a cause where you see a problem in the world around you. There are plenty to choose from, and this takes the onus off of you and directs this same energy into a worthy cause.

Saturn to the Nodes

Conjunct Your North Node

Your path of soul growth is linked to your path of self-mastery. The more you internalize your relationship to authority and demonstrate this with some type of self-control, self-restraint, and self-discipline, the more you are on your path of soul growth. Without an internal sense of authority, you will view anything connected to soul growth as burdensome and heavy.

Conjunct Your South Node

You come into this life with karma connected to the right use of authoritative power. It is as if you had used executive power effectively, but not compassionately, in a previous life. This might help explain why you run up against uncaring administrative bureaucracy in your life. Learn the lesson of how to be more compassionate with your power, and you pass the test. In relationships, this aspect can manifest as a tendency to slide into commitment and contract as the basis of the relationship, while neglecting the romantic side.

Harmonious to Both Nodes

Your natural way of handling responsibility is right on track with your soul growth. You have integrated a discipline for staying on your path that has become almost second nature for you. You have the gift of patience with your spiritual path, and you incorporate what you learn along the way.

Square Both Nodes

Until you resolve your issues with authority, you are likely to have difficulty both with people from your past and with staying on your path of soul growth. Ask yourself where you give authority away to others in needless resistance and judgment. It is like judging your own path. You can't learn from the material if you can't accept the material. Once you identify this resistance to your own path as your chief stumbling block, you can start the process of taking responsibility for your life and your choices. This allows you to work through your issues rather than against them.

21
Uranus Through the Houses and Signs

Uranus symbolizes the urge for freedom and independence. The house and sign where Uranus is in your chart will be an area of life where you are meant to cast off social and cultural conditioning to discover your authentic self. This can be expressed as a radical urge to do things your own way in the matters of the house and sign it is in. It is where you can't go with convention—you can fight against it, or invent your own way, but you simply just can't go with convention. This is where your soul seeks discovery to stay on the path of evolutionary awakening.

> *Note:* The outer planets take so long to complete their orbits that they spend years in a particular sign (Uranus—7 years, Neptune—13 years, and Pluto—up to 20 years); thus their influence spreads out over an entire generation of people. The house an outer planet occupies in your chart is where you will have the greatest personal experience of the collective influence of its sign. Because of this, only the house placement of the outer planets will be presented here.

Uranus in the First House

Liberating Influence

Here, the radical urge for individuality will have a strong impact on your personality. You are here to liberate yourself from all restraints that hold you back from expressing your authentic personality.

Impact on Relationships

Uranus won't let you compromise your freedom in any way, so you will need to learn how to express your individuality in an uncompromising way within a relationship. If you see commitment and freedom as mutually exclusive, Uranus will always demand the freedom. You need a relationship that allows you considerable room for individual expression; otherwise, there will be trouble in paradise.

Uranus in the Second House

Liberating Influence

You need to cast off your culture's attitude about security to discover your authentic self in all issues related to money and security. You are here to trust in your ability to be innovative to provide for yourself and to cultivate your unique talents and interests into marketable skills.

Impact on Relationships

If you are at the stage of fighting for your right to be free with money-related issues, it would make cooperating in the financial issues of a relationship difficult. If you have successfully liberated yourself from the cultural neurosis about security, you won't feel your independence threatened in close relationships; your independent sense of security comes with you.

Uranus in the Third House

Liberating Influence

Here, the liberating influence of Uranus deals with the mind, what you think about and how you express your ideas. You are meant to break free of cultural learning expectations to pursue your independent interests.

Impact on Relationships

The low road with this placement would make communications in relationships difficult. Uranus is disruptive and makes it difficult to listen and to accept the ideas and opinions of others as valid. The high road is when you have cultivated patience in letting others form their ideas at their own pace. Then your brilliant insights and fresh perspective are welcomed by others.

Uranus in the Fourth House

Liberating Influence

You are meant to cast off the attitudes and experiences of home, house, and family you received from your culture and family of origin. You are meant to be a bit of a black sheep in order to discover what authentically works for you to create sanctuary for yourself.

Impact on Relationships

The unexpected events that Uranus is known for in the Fourth House of home and family make it difficult to establish roots and a secure family life. You are not meant to fit into the cultural archetype that works for others. When you are honoring your authentic needs for retreat and creating sanctuary for yourself, then you can find the right partner to share your unique lifestyle.

Uranus in the Fifth House

Liberating Influence

The liberating influence of Uranus in your Fifth House of creative self-expression will show you breaking free of other people's ideas concerning fun, play, children, romance, and creativity. This is where you need to allow your authentic individuality to express itself in your own unique way.

Impact on Relationships

The Fifth House deals with the romantic and courtship phase of a relationship. With this placement, you crave the excitement of romance, and if it dies down in a relationship, your interest will wander. If you are with someone you would like to stay with, be an innovative lover and keep the discovery of romance alive by always inventing new ways to court each other.

Uranus in the Sixth House

Liberating Influence

With this placement, you will need to cast off your culture's attitudes concerning work, health, and your daily routines. It is essential to find the work that allows you to do things your own unique way. The same goes with health: be willing to explore and discover a health program that fits your unique needs.

Impact on Relationships

Your dietary needs and how you carry out your daily routines are likely different from the norm. Because of this, it would favorable for you to be with a person who understands your need for a daily schedule that allows you some freedom. You are not the best in a joined-at-the-hip type of relationship; you would find yourself trying to find some free time alone.

Uranus in the Seventh House

Liberating Influence

You are not meant to fit into society-defined relationships; you are looking for something different. You need to experiment a bit in different types of relationships, and there is likely to be something unusual about relationships you do get involved in. You need to align with the evolutionary, awakening energy of Uranus through your relationships.

Impact on Relationships

Your need for freedom in the Seventh House of relationships presents a tall order. It could lead to a lifelong series of intense relationships that abruptly end when they become routine. If you find someone you want to stay with, you must always introduce new opportunities for growth into the relationship, or you know what will happen. You need an evolutionary-based relationship that serves both of your individual needs for soul growth and expression, and continues to evolve into new forms itself.

Uranus in the Eighth House

Liberating Influence

You need to liberate yourself from cultural attitudes about sexuality to discover your authentic interests for intimacy. You are innovative as a lover and thrive on the excitement of sexual discovery; however, the sticky, sentimental attachment that often comes with intimacy would be something you would strongly resist.

Impact on Relationships

Your passions run hot and cold. You are a marvelous lover when there is discovery and exploration, but Uranus resists attachments, and as soon as you feel the closeness of intimacy, you recoil from the resulting attachment. At a higher level, you may have the ability to work with the kundalini energy awakened in sexuality and can experience all of your chakras opening in love's embrace.

Uranus in the Ninth House

Liberating Influence

You need to liberate yourself from the religious, political, and philosophical beliefs of your culture to discover your authentic guiding beliefs. You are meant to challenge everybody, including yourself, to think for themselves and not be a robot to the beliefs of others.

Impact on Relationships

The low road of this placement would lead to arguments in your relationships rooted in your need to challenge your partner's opinions and views about education, politics, religion, and philosophical issues. The high road opens up when you have liberated yourself from the need to challenge every viewpoint that is different than yours. Then you can establish a relationship where you and your partner are both constantly rediscovering truth; exploring everything, accepting nothing, and challenging each other to constantly look at life with a fresh perspective.

Uranus in the Tenth House

Liberating Influence

You are here to cast off your culture's attitudes about success and in some way demonstrate your uniqueness and originality in your career pursuits. You can't be confined to someone else's image of what you should be doing with your life, or your time.

Impact on Relationships

The best match for you would be a partner who isn't concerned with convention and what other people think. You are certainly not interested in your social reputation, and it would be ideal to be with a partner who enjoys this about you. Then the two of you together could flaunt convention where you believe things need to be shaken up a bit.

Uranus in the Eleventh House

Liberating Influence

This is Uranus' natural house, and this placement awakens the call for social activism. This is not as much personal as cultural; you see where your culture has to change to meet the needs of the times. You are a catalyst for others in awakening them to social issues that need addressing.

Impact on Relationships

You would do best with a partner who also likes to explore the edge of what is socially acceptable. You need the friendship level of your relationship to be vital, challenging each other always to be authentic in social pursuits, and yet sentimental friendship feels restricting. To align with a partner who shares, or at least supports, your views on social activism would be ideal.

Uranus in the Twelfth House

Liberating Influence

You are here to liberate yourself from your culture's attitudes about mystical and spiritual realms. You will likely have experiences that do not fit with what you have been trained to believe possible. This may cause you deep concern about your mental well-being, or you could liberate yourself from the limiting attitudes of your culture and go with your authentic mystical experiences.

Impact on Relationships

You are more like an icebreaker with other people's frozen emotional karma than a compassionate and understanding friend. You would do best with a partner who is not timid about spiritual growth, as you tend to cut through your own and other people's spiritual baggage. A timid partner would find you insensitive and lacking compassion for the wounds of the past.

22
Neptune Through the Houses and Signs

Neptune symbolizes the urge for transcendence. It describes your imagination, which can lead to inspirations or illusions; it is your blind spot.

Neptune's influence is otherworldly. The urge associated with Neptune is to transcend the pressures of the everyday world through the imagination. Neptune's function is essentially spiritual; its job is to dissolve the separate ego identity where it is in your chart so that you can align with a larger transcendent reality, beyond the ego. This is where you could align with the Buddhist concept of "no self," allowing the higher spiritual energies to move through you. The artist, the spiritual seeker, and the romantic are all using the Neptune imagination in a way that enhances their lives with inspiration.

Neptune can also lead to illusions and escapism of various types that cause nothing but trouble. This happens when the ego distorts the Neptune imagination to serve the needs of the ego. In relationships, Neptune can inspire you, or delude you, depending on how skillful you are at navigating the subtle realms it deals with. Look up the house where Neptune falls in your chart to see where this inspirational/blind-spot energy is operating in your life.

Neptune in the First House

The high road of this placement leads to you knowing how to connect with that which inspires you, and you bring this inspirational energy into your relationships. When the ego dissolves, as it will with this placement, that indicates that you have learned to skillfully align with the higher spiritual and creative energy that flows through you. The low road is when your identity is dissolved, but you haven't found a healthy creative or spiritual outlet. Then it is time for an identity meltdown, with no inspiration to back it up. You would then be vulnerable to accepting anyone else's definition of who you should be, since you don't have your own identity.

Neptune in the Second House

The high road of this placement leads to inspirational attitudes about the right use of resources, and you can inspire your partner toward a visionary attitude about money. You are meant to find your security through your faith more than your pocketbook. The low road leads to Neptune's blind spot with money issues, which is notorious for seeing financial potential and value that just isn't there. You should check all of your ideas and plans concerning money and security issues with your partner before you sign on the dotted line.

Neptune in the Third House

With Neptune in the Third House of communication, you take conversations beyond the trivial and into what inspires you. Your imagination can soar above petty issues in the house of the everyday mind. Your blind spot comes from this same transcending of the details. It is best for you to get all of your agreements with others in writing with your imagination in the house of communication . . . was it said, or imagined? Transcending the details of everyday life is grand for the poet, but in your relationships, this can be a source of aggravation.

Neptune in the Fourth House

The high road of this placement leads to transcending your family-of-origin experience of home and family to live out your own vision. With Neptune at the bottom of your chart, you are meant to connect to your inspirational source in private. Nature can be a source of inspiration for you. In a relationship, you would benefit from a partner who acknowledges your need for tranquility in the home environment. The low road leads to dissolved foundations, giving a feeling of groundlessness, like there is nothing beneath you to support you. Your early home life could have left you feeling confused as to your foundations rather than secure, and this erodes your ability to create your own nest until you disengage from your early-family myth and discover your own.

Neptune in the Fifth House

This is one of the best and worst places for Neptune, depending on your skill in handling your imagination in the Fifth House of play. This is the house of creative self-expression and is quite a playground for your imagination. Neptune's influence on the romantic issues of the Fifth House is both delightful and disastrous! It is delightful when this fanciful placement for dancing and romancing is supported by a relationship that is grounded in all other areas of life; but it is disastrous when romance is the only basis for the relationship, or worse, when you fall prey to illusions and deception in the name of romance.

Neptune in the Sixth House

The high road with this placement is when you have found a way to be of service to others without becoming a servant. Your health is more sensitive than most to viruses, allergies, toxins, and the like, but you have learned to adjust your diet to accommodate your sensitivity. Incorporating meditation and prayer into your health regime would be helpful. The low road leads to difficulty staying focused on your daily routines—you get lost in your imagination and just daydream the day away. You may also have to face all kinds of neurotic fears that your imagination conjures up concerning your health. Until you cultivate a healthy use of your imagination and train it toward positive imagery, it will randomly erode your confidence with periodic bouts of fear.

Neptune in the Seventh House

The notorious blind spot of Neptune in the Seventh House of relationships shows you to be vulnerable to falling in love with your partner's potential, and ignoring the actual person. The disillusionment that follows is predictable. Here is a rule to follow to avoid this cycle: Before you get involved in any serious relationship, business or romantic, pull back and ask yourself, "Am I attracted to the qualities of this relationship in the here-and-now reality, or am I attracted to the potential of how things could be?" Ignoring these questions could be disastrous. You do best in relationships with those who have mastered a healthy expression of their imagination, and who are *not* looking for someone to believe in them to get over their troubles.

Neptune in the Eighth House

Weaving your imagination into the Eighth House of intimacy creates all sorts of interesting opportunities to enhance a relationship. You can be a very imaginative and sensitive lover. At a high level, you are aware of chakras and the subtle bodies and their role in intimacy. This could lead to interests in sexual magic, sacred sexuality, and tantra sexuality as opportunities to enhance your relationship. The low road can lead to addictive sexual fantasies. There is nothing wrong with fantasy, unless it becomes a substitute for the real thing. You would be avoiding the emotional transformations that occur through risking intimacy with another. The trick is to integrate your imagination into your love life, not replace it. Neptune's blind spot in the Eighth House of shared resources calls for extra caution in all financial dealing with others. Contracts are a must to bring clarity to agreements that could otherwise get clouded with illusions.

Neptune in the Ninth House

Your imagination can soar into the abstract realms of the Ninth House to gain inspiration from the spiritual teachings and teachers from many traditions. Finding the teachings that feed your soul is the quest, and questing into the spiritual mystery traditions is very satisfying for you. You will seek a partner to share the lofty ideals and principles that guide you in relationships. The low road comes when you are so eager to believe in something that you become vulnerable to false teachings and false gurus who lead you away from your inner connection to spirit. Other misuses of this placement could lead to spiritual arrogance in relationships, or other forms of getting lost in glamorizing the spiritual path.

Neptune in the Tenth House

You are not just looking for a job or a career with this placement—you want to know your soul's purpose. You can draw inspiration from careers that involve artistic or altruistic pursuits, satisfying your soul and not just your pocketbook. This inspires others to reach for loftier ambitions in their lives as well. The low road leads to all types of dreams of what you might do someday; but they can become escapist fantasies, with no real plans, unless you train your imagination to enhance your professional life rather than replace it.

Neptune in the Eleventh House

The high road with this placement leads to the social visionary, joining with others for compassionate, altruistic causes. You also can draw true inspiration from your friendships and social gatherings that involve music and dance. The low road shows that you can too easily be lead astray by the wrong friends. You also imagine potential in friendships that others can't live up to, which ultimately leads to disillusionment. This cycle continues until you realize that it is your illusions that are letting you down, not your friends. Seeing your friends' potential is beautiful, but you need to balance this with absolute acceptance of where they are at in the here-and-now world, to avoid Neptune's blind spot.

Neptune in the Twelfth House

This is Neptune's natural house, and the high road gives you direct access to the "still, small voice within." With this direct connection to your spiritual source, you are always able to return to your own inner guidance when you are in need. Dreams, journaling, using the oracles, and quality time alone always bring you home. A relationship with a partner who shares these spiritual sensitivities would be ideal. Your partner learns to trust your intuition when your alarms go off regarding any of your partner's dealings with others in the world. When your imagination is not skillfully handled, you are prone to absorb the neurotic fears of the world, thinking they are yours. You can get lost in endless wanderings of the planet of imagination, until you get it: the source you seek is within you, period.

23
Pluto Through the Houses and Signs

Pluto describes the subconscious qualities that must be purged in order to experience true intimacy. It is the destiny you came to act out in the big picture of life, and where you are being tested with the right use of power.

Pluto takes 249 years to complete its journey through the zodiac; thus it connects you to patterns of behavior that are larger than this one life. It is one of the clues in your chart of the nature of the past-life karma you brought into this life. Pluto represents your soul memories, deeply embedded within your subconscious, of issues you have been working on for many lifetimes. Pluto's home in mythology is the underworld, thus it represents your shadow qualities, the less than honorable aspect of your human nature that all humans must face. Specifically, your Pluto house is where you need to purge controlling, manipulating behavior so that you can participate in the larger role you came here to perform, beyond simply serving your own ego needs.

Pluto in the First House

You are being tested with the right use of the power of your personality. You need to use your power in such a way as to benefit the world and not just yourself. To do this, you must first purge the purely self-serving ego in order to become a vehicle for the collective will. Your natural leadership ability can coalesce a group of divergent people into a consolidated unit at work, home, or in the community. In relationships, this will manifest as difficulty in cooperative endeavors when you are in the clutches of the shadow.

Pluto in the Second House

You are being tested with the right use of the power of your resources. You are meant to experience transformation in how you earn and spend your money, from self-serving to benefiting humanity. The shadow side is becoming obsessive, or even ruthless, in acquiring resources, and it is not unusual for this behavior to lead to wealth. The high road is typified by the attitude "The more money I acquire, the more I can give to those in need." When you are gripped by the shadow, this will manifest as periodic difficulties over money issues in relationships.

Pluto in the Third House

You are being tested with the right use of the power of your mind. Your probing intellect sees beneath the surface of superficial information and gets to the causal level of what is going on in any situation. Students, researchers, writers, and investigators would benefit from this relentless intellectual intensity. The shadow side manifests if you do not provide healthy intellectual food for your rapacious mind, which won't go hungry. You could become obsessed about neurotic issues, or worse, plan revenge over wrongs done to you. In relationships, your penetrating insights add profoundness to your conversations, but when you are in the grips of the shadow, your insights can be cruel.

Pluto in the Fourth House

You are being tested with the right use of power in your home and family. You need to totally transform your early experience with family and society into that which can be meaningful for you in creating your roots. It is not unlikely that destiny arranged for you to be born into a family that was unhealthy and unable to provide for your needs.

The shadow comes out when you are unable to purge this early conditioning, and then either can't create home and family for yourself because it is just too wounding, or worse, you create family but pass on the unhealthy traditions of your youth. Deep within you, beyond the wounds, your soul knows what a healthy family life would be for you; trust this.

Pluto in the Fifth House

You are being tested with the right use of the power of your creative expression. You will need to transform the attitudes about creativity and celebrating life that you received growing up. The shadow side of your character can manifest as an obsessive indulgence in drugs, alcohol, or sex in an attempt to lose yourself in the pursuit of pleasure. Deep within you is a reservoir of creative energy ready to be tapped when you purge yourself of the addictive quest for pleasure. Your higher purpose is to live a life aligned with your heart and to demonstrate the power of pursuing love as opposed to the love of pursuing power.

Pluto in the Sixth House

You are being tested with the right use of the power of your work, in the world and on yourself. The Sixth House is where you critically analyze yourself to see what can be improved. The shadow can manifest as brutal self-assessment, leading to feelings of worthlessness. The ego is meant to be subdued in the Sixth House, but not annihilated. You are here to transform these inhibiting attitudes of self-loathing into a constructive evaluation of where you could further your skill development in order to be of service to others.

Pluto in the Seventh House

You are being tested with the right use of power in your relationships. The impact that you have on others is far greater than you ever intend, and your work is to purge any tendencies you have to abuse this influence. If you deny your power in relationships, you will attract controlling, domineering, or manipulative people into your life. Another form of denial is to avoid participating in relationships, deeming them to be too volatile, which effectively removes you from the growth and transformations that occur through deep involvement with others. Having seen the darker side of relationships, the shadow can manifest as an inability to fully trust others. You are here to purge all manipulative behavior from your relationships and to use your power to help bring honor and integrity to all of your dealings with others.

Pluto in the Eighth House

This is Pluto's natural house, and its impact on sex, shared resources, and death will be at its strongest here; you are being tested with the right use of power in these areas. Destiny will bring you experiences that lay bare the depravity and corruption of the human spirit as your preparation for one-on-one, intimate relationships. Because of these perverse encounters, you are not a goody-goody and nothing about anybody could ever shock you. This does distort your lens for allowing intimacy into your life by creating a desperateness to your love. Yes, your soul is desperate for the healing waters of intimacy, but being desperate blocks the very intimacy you seek, and will bring instead only phantasms of repressed desires. You need to purge yourself of this dark-side conditioning, and follow that voice deep within you that knows it is simply love that you need to give and receive to experience the innocence of intimacy.

Pluto in the Ninth House

You are being tested with the right use of the power of your persuasion. You are a master in the realm of philosophical debate. Destiny will reveal to you the dark side of religion and politics, and your shadow side comes out as the cynic, discounting everyone's beliefs. You need to experience a transformation of the ethnocentricity that you are exposed to early in life by exploring other cultures and their beliefs through travel and education. You then seem to be called on to help others confront their biases, prejudices, and narrow thinking and expand to adopt a more inclusive worldview.

Pluto in the Tenth House

You are being tested with the right use of the power of your position in the world. With the Tenth House at the top of the chart, people look up to you in ways you don't always understand, and it is part of your soul path to use this influence in ways that benefit the world and not just yourself. Destiny will place you in situations where you will see the misuse of power and reputation, either in your family or your culture. You are in your shadow when you either deny your public power, or ruthlessly seize the power and misuse it for personal gain. Your job is to transform this fear, or obsession, with power, and do something meaningful with the position of influence you have been given.

Pluto in the Eleventh House

You are being tested with the right use of the power of your friendships and social alliances. The Eleventh House is where the "I" becomes part of the "We" of humanity. Destiny will arrange for you to be confronted with the dark side of humanity, which manifests as elitism and favoritism benefiting certain groups and excluding others. You are in your shadow when you believe that humanity is not worth the effort and it is better just to watch out for your own interests. You are here to purge these self-serving attitudes and join with other like-minded souls who are attempting to make the world a better place.

Pluto in the Twelfth House

You are being tested with the right use of the power of your spirituality. The Twelfth House is the direct connection to spirit through the compassionate heart. Destiny will put you in situations where you are taught that numbing and avoidance are the best ways to deal with human suffering of any kind. You are in your shadow when you feel there is just too much pain in the world and it is best not to let it in or it will overwhelm you. You are here to transform this denial and open your heart to the suffering in the world. Of course, if you carry this suffering as a martyr, it is just another mask of the shadow. You could benefit by learning the art of feeling the pain in the world, blessing it, and laying it on the lap of God.

24
The North Node/South Node Axis Through the Houses and Signs

The North Node and South Node are always exactly opposite each other and form an axis of incarnation. The South Node is where you have inherited understanding from your own past lives. It is also the path of least resistance and no growth, because you have already covered this material. The North Node is the path your soul seeks for growth in this life.

North Node in Aries or the First House/
South Node in Libra or the Seventh House

Your path of soul growth is to develop the courage to stand up for your own choices. The path of least resistance is to seek approval from others. You developed this habit in past lives, and you are skilled at pleasing others in this life because of it. But the path of growth is in trusting your instincts enough to take independent action.

North Node in Taurus or the Second House/
South Node in Scorpio or the Eighth House

Your path of soul growth is to provide for yourself abundantly through developing your own skills and talents. The path of least resistance is to rely on others for support. You developed this deep rapport with your partner for your security in a previous life, and can easily attract support in this life. But if this leads to co-dependency, you are cut off from your growth, which comes from developing your personal ability to provide for your security.

North Node in Gemini or the Third House/
South Node in Sagittarius or the Ninth House

Your path of soul growth is to stay open-minded and inquisitive about all aspects of life. Your path of least resistance is to become so intent on what you perceive to be true that you run the risk of becoming dogmatic and prejudiced. This strong sense of moral conviction, which you have brought with you from past lives, gives you strong skills in philosophical, religious, and political debates. However, when winning the argument becomes more important than stretching your views to entertain differences of opinion, you have cut yourself off from your path of growth.

North Node in Cancer or the Fourth House/
South Node in Capricorn or the Tenth House

Your path of soul growth is to cultivate your roots and learn to draw on your personal life of home, house, and family for emotional sustenance. Your path of least resistance is to constantly tend to your social life and career for your identity. You have brought an understanding of how to be successful forward from previous lives and can easily find all the social and professional success you want in this life. But if success prevents you from having time to develop your personal life, you have been cut off from your path of growth.

North Node in Leo or the Fifth House/
South Node in Aquarius or the Eleventh House

Your path of soul growth is to pursue a life aligned with your heart, develop your personality, have some fun, and express yourself creatively. Your path of least resistance is to become so dedicated to a cause or larger social concern that you hardly have time for your personal life. You have been a champion of just causes in previous lives and can easily give yourself over to a worthy issue in this life. But if this squeezes out time for personal play, fun, creativity, and romance, you have cut yourself off of your path of growth.

North Node in Virgo or the Sixth House/
South Node in Pisces or the Twelfth House

Your path of soul growth in this life is to find a way to be of service in your day-to-day life and to develop a proactive approach to the health of your body. Your path of least resistance is to escape the details and humdrum of everyday existence to dream of a much more imaginative life. You have experienced long periods of retreat in previous lives and are quite comfortable alone in your inner world in this life. But if this prohibits you from developing skills for getting involved and pitching in with the day-to-day world, you are cut off from your path of growth.

North Node in Libra or the Seventh House/
South Node in Aries or the First House

Your path of soul growth is to cultivate beauty and refinement in your life and also to develop your relationship skills to cooperatively live with others. Your path of least resistance is to live independently from others and to trust your own instincts for direction. You have been highly independent in your previous lives and can easily manage on your own. But if this prevents you from developing the negotiating skills on which all cooperation is based, you have been cut off from your path of growth.

North Node in Scorpio or the Eighth House/ South Node in Taurus or the Second House

Your path of soul growth is to take the emotional risk involved in opening up to intimacy and passion. Your path of least resistance is to stay within your own comfort zone for material security and not risk anything that might disrupt this security. You have had abundance in previous lives and can easily isolate yourself with material security in this life. But if this holds you back from putting your emotional vulnerability on the line for the sake of passion and emotional intimacy, you have been cut off from your growth.

North Node in Sagittarius or the Ninth House/ South Node in Gemini or the Third House

Your path of soul growth is to cultivate the attitude of the adventurer, exploring through travel, higher education, and philosophical pursuits an ever-expanding search for truth. Your path of least resistance is to dabble in this and that, pursuing whatever fascinates you in the moment. You have been a dilettante in previous lives, open-minded but not directed, and you can easily fit into a carefree lifestyle. But if in this endless exploring of options you never settle on goals that expand your life, you are cut off from your growth.

North Node in Capricorn or the Tenth House/ South Node in Cancer or the Fourth House

Your path of soul growth is to cultivate your career, to rise to the heights, and in slow steady steps, to make something of yourself. Your path of least resistance is in avoiding responsibility for career and worldly issues, and instead seeking comfort in your personal life of home, house, and family. You have had a rich family life in your most recent life and can easily attract a lifestyle deeply enmeshed in family issues in this life. But if this limits your ability to strive to do something significant with your life, you have been cut off from your growth.

North Node in Aquarius or the Eleventh House/ South Node in Leo or the Fifth House

Your path of soul growth is to find a meaningful connection to the society around you and, through friendships and getting involved in larger social concerns, to find a way to make the world a better place. Your path of least resistance is to get so caught up in your personal life and creative pursuits that there is no time for meaningful social involvement. The past-life tendency that you bring into this life is that of a special, favored individual, with some type of star status. You have a knack for attracting a life of much fun with room for personal expression as well. However, if this doesn't allow time for expanding your social horizons and getting involved in some type of altruistic cause, you are cut off from your path of growth.

North Node in Pisces or the Twelfth House/ South Node in Virgo or the Sixth House

Your path of soul growth is to cultivate faith in the guidance you receive by trusting in a reality beyond your ego. Maintaining a compassionate heart for the true feelings and emotions of others is also central to your path. Your path of least resistance is to get on with the business of taking care of the practical details of your life. Your past-life legacy is that of a task-oriented perfectionist who had it together because you kept it together, and you can easily develop a life guided by this worker-bee mentality again. However, if you get so lost in the tasks of life that you miss the beauty, the poetry, and the mystery of life, you have cut yourself off from your path of growth.

Part Three
Synastry—The Art of Chart Comparison

Now that you have thoroughly explored your own relationship profile, it is time to compare your chart with someone else's for compatibility. You will want to have both people's birth charts, plus charts called "biwheels" with each person's planets placed around each other's birth chart, and finally a synastry table showing every major aspect from each person's planets to each of the other's planets. Yes, this is a ton of information, and to the newcomer to astrology it can seem overwhelming. But have heart: this book provides a system to complete all the important evaluations and make some sense of it all.

I like to start with the most general views and then focus in on details as I progress. First, look into each chart with a relationship filter to see what general issues surround each person concerning relationships. Then take a look at the big picture of each chart. Is there a complement or reiteration of hemispheric emphasis? How do the elements and qualities match? Do they complement or reiterate each other?

Next, look at the major aspects in both charts. It is not uncommon to see a theme, i.e., one person has Pluto conjunct Sun and the other has Pluto opposite Sun. You will see a surprising number of ties like this when you start exploring relationship charts. When you see a theme between the two charts, this is always going to represent a dominant theme in the relationship. The theme of Pluto with the Sun, as in our example, would lead to power and control issues. There would likely be a compelling passion that would draw the two people together, but sooner or later these control issues will surface.

Keep an eye out for what are called "accidental conjunctions." For example, one person has Moon in Leo in the Seventh House and the other has Moon in Taurus in the Fifth House. Normally, Leo and Taurus are not an easy combination, but the Taurus Moon falling in the Fifth House adds a Leo flavor to it, and this accidental conjunction can lead to many shared experiences that are mutually rewarding. Paying attention to these accidental conjunctions will reveal possible connections that otherwise would not have been seen.

I then like to compare each planet of one person's chart to the same planet in the other, showing similarities and differences in basic life responses. In the next chapter, interpretations are offered for the major aspects with each other, but you will want to keep in mind the conditions concerning the planet in each chart. Is it well aspected, or does it have many challenges in its own chart? The planets are not isolated in the chart; they are part of a pattern and must be considered as such.

25
Same Planet Comparison

With this first level of same planet comparison, I recommend dropping the degrees and orbs altogether and simply considering the aspects by the signs the planets are in. Of course, the closer the aspect is to exact, the more pronounced the influence will be.

Your Sun to Partner's Sun

Conjunction

This leads to a strong sense of recognition, a feeling of something deeply familiar. It is one of the best ties for friendships and working relationships. However, for romantic relationships, it is important not to take each other for granted—too much familiarity is a sure killer of magnetism.

Harmonious

Your basic life energies are in natural harmony with each other, making it easy to be supportive of one another and feel at ease in each other's company.

Challenging

Your basic life energies are naturally at odds with each other. Therefore, you tend to compete and fall into patterns of putting each other down, rather than supporting each other. To have a healthy relationship, you both are forced to stretch your acceptance of the differences in each other.

Your Moon to Partner's Moon

This is one of the ready indicators of compatibility in analyzing charts; the Moon is that important in relationships. How you both express your emotions, your comfort zone, the habits you are drawn to in order to retreat, the type of living environment that you thrive in—all of these are hugely important in relationships.

Harmonious (including conjunction)

Your emotional styles are compatible, allowing you both to feel you can be yourselves. Even the way you experience "downtime" is in harmony, so you can rejuvenate in each other's presence. You speak the same emotional language and likely feel that you "get" each other at a deep level.

Challenging

Your emotional needs are at odds with each other, as are the ways in which you both express your emotions, making emotional communication difficult. The challenge is to allow enough space in the relationship for both of you to get your individual needs met. That is the high road. Even if you have learned to accommodate for these differences, it is still wise to allow some time apart on a daily basis so you can drop into that place of just being yourself.

Your Mercury to Partner's Mercury

This impacts all mental-related activity in the relationship, including communication styles, what you both tend to think about, and how you process information before making decisions together.

Harmonious (including conjunction)

It is easy to understand each other, as your minds work in similar styles. Making decisions together is supported, and when communication difficulties do arise, they are readily resolved when there is the intention to do so.

Challenging

You both have to give each other space to come to your decisions in your own way. Your minds aren't always on the same page—what each of you thinks is important, and how you communicate this isn't always well received by the other. There are millions of great relationships with Mercury at odds with each other, but these are always people who have learned how to avoid judging each other's perceptions. That is the high road.

Your Venus to Partner's Venus

With Venus, you compare how your tastes align in terms of love, beauty, art, and of course romance. This will show how you both receive love and pleasure, as well as what you would like to share with another.

Harmonious (including conjunction)

Your values and tastes in life are in harmony and this makes it easy to enjoy each other's company. From music, to food, to love's sweet embrace, you find many ways to enjoy your life together.

Challenging

Your values and your tastes are at odds with each other. This often creates magnetism, but issues concerning different values will likely have to be ironed out. You need to allow enough space in the relationship to allow for your different tastes.

Your Mars to Partner's Mars

With Mars, you compare how you assert yourselves, take action, define your boundaries, and act on your passions and frustrations.

Conjunction

Since you both apply yourselves in the same way and basically do things the same way, this most often leads to natural harmony. However, this also leads to the two-roosters-in-the-same-barnyard scenario whenever pecking-order issues arise.

Harmonious

The way that you naturally go about doing things flows with one another. No matter how fired up either of you gets, you still do not readily provoke each other's defenses. It seems to be easy to avoid conflicts and resolve them when they arise.

Challenging

This is one of the red flags to watch out for in comparing charts. Your energies tend to conflict, particularly if either of you attempts to correct the other's actions. This is a passionate aspect, which is wonderful in certain arenas, but can also lead to passionate arguments. You can only be at ease with each other to the degree that you can accept the differences in how you both go about doing things. Otherwise, there tends to be conflict over everything. Learning to avoid expressing yourself to each other when your solar plexus is tight would help immensely. When your solar plexus is tight, your partner hears whatever you are saying as a punch. Harness the power, and great things can be accomplished with your combined energy; otherwise, petty arguments and disagreements rule the day.

Your Jupiter to Partner's Jupiter

This impacts how you both reach for goals and your philosophical orientations that either support or conflict with one another. Jupiter shows your natural styles for being generous in your relationship.

Harmonious (including conjunction)

You will have plenty of opportunities to find mutually rewarding activities. Your philosophies about living life support one another. Traveling, education, and spiritual explorations all provide avenues of growth for the relationship.

Challenging

Since what each of you finds rewarding is at odds, you need to create enough space in your relationship for both of you to take part in the separate activities that you each find rewarding. There could be disagreements over each other's political, religious, or philosophical beliefs.

Your Saturn to Partner's Saturn

Saturn represents some of the biggest challenges we face in life and obviously is critically important in relationships. Saturn represents the nature of the fears, insecurities, and challenges we face on the way to becoming our own authority in life. In comparing two people's Saturns, you want to look for how they support each other's difficulties. Saturn is most readily seen as projection in relationships—the issues we have the most difficulty with in others are the very same issues we have difficulty accepting in ourselves; thus we project onto others what we dislike in ourselves. If you know this is going on, you can read into your projected dislikes as reflections of where you need more self-control, self-restraint, and self-discipline. This is always what Saturn asks of us: self-mastery, that's all!

Saturn is a builder, and if you are successful in supporting each other's Saturn issues, you can bring the perseverance, patience, and determination that Saturn provides at its best into your relationship.

Conjunction

There are no dominance and submission issues between the two of you, because you have absolutely equal power to stand up to each other. You will have to negotiate all issues between the two of you, as neither of you will allow the other to get away with any power trips. You can be very supportive and helpful toward each other in times of challenge, because your strategies for dealing with difficult situations are right on track with each other.

Harmonious

You solve life's difficult situations in a supportive manner, allowing you to appreciate each other's help and assistance. You are able to learn from life together, and thus can avoid making the same mistakes over and over again.

Challenging

This aspect is another red flag in comparison astrology. This is a set-up for disappointment if you don't allow for the differences. The effect is most noticeable in how you both handle each other's "bad day" scenarios. When one of you is having a bad day and is venting insecurities and problems, and the other person offers what seems to be good and caring advice, it often offends the person with the security issues, and the other person gets upset over not being appreciated for having offered help . . . the set-up for disappointment. To avoid this scenario, learn this one rule: On these bad days when your partner is expressing concerns, learn to listen more and talk less. You eventually learn that your best ideas are not well received anyway, so work on patience and silent emotional support and you'll avoid unnecessary grief.

The Outer Planets

These planets spend so many years in the same sign that it is common to find them in the same signs in charts you are comparing. When they are in different signs, then it is important to explore the differences to better understand the impact on the relationship. Otherwise, it is almost best to think of these as generational planets—a whole generation is born with the same combination. To determine the impact of these transpersonal planets on the individual, look for house placement and aspects to other planets. This will give you specific information on how the collective theme is working through the individual.

Pay close attention to when outer planets are in aspect to personal planets, as this will always have a strong impact on the personality, particularly the challenging aspects. The outer planets deal with forces that are larger than the individual ego can control, thus the individual is wrestling with forces larger than the self. This will always have an impact on relationships, and every other area of life.

However, just because there is a challenging aspect from an outer planet to a personal planet in a chart does not necessarily mean this is troublesome in the person's life. It would probably start out that way, as all challenging aspects do, but many people with challenging outer planet aspects are advanced souls, and many are not. Will the individual accept the challenge of the outer planets, which is to evolve and grow in consciousness beyond the ego? Or will the individual anchor himself or herself in the bastion of the ego identity and do battle with the invading forces of the outer planets? These answers are not shown in the chart. Consciousness growth is an individual matter; some people take the step and some don't. You'll have to observe the individual's life outside the chart to see if he or she is working with the outer planets, or against them.

26
Your Characters in
Your Partner's Theater

When you put your planets in your partner's chart and vice versa, you see where you impact each other, for good or ill. The nature of your planet activates the theme of the house where it falls in your partner's chart. Let's say you have your Sun at 15° Virgo in your chart. If your partner has 5° Virgo on the Fifth House cusp, then your Sun will be in your partner's Fifth House, bringing your vitality and life force into your partner's house of romance, fun, and creative self-expression.

Sun in Each Other's Houses

The Sun represents your life force, and where this falls in your partner's chart is where your vital life force will have a positive, animating impact on your partner's life.

Your Sun in Partner's First House

You animate the most physical and direct sense of identity for your partner. He or she feels your strong support, and can even feel physically stronger when you are together.

With this placement, you inspire confidence in your partner to stand up and be counted. All shared physical activities are empowered, including lovemaking.

Your Sun in Partner's Second House

You inspire a sense of confidence in your partner's ability to rise to the occasion of providing for himself or herself. Your partner feels secure with you. You both get actively involved in each other's issues about money—how to earn it and how to spend it. This activates mutual enjoyment of sensual experiences, from food and music to the bedroom.

Your Sun in Partner's Third House

You illuminate your partner's mind and keep the flow of communication animated between the two of you. You like to stay informed, even of the daily details of your partner's life. You can stimulate all types of mutual interests in learning, from books, to classes, to computers, to all other sources of information.

Sun in Partner's Fourth House

The Fourth House is your partner's deepest place within himself or herself. Your Sun here shows that you animate that deepest place within your partner. You touch the place within your partner that feels like home. This is a good placement for people living together, as your partner feels safe to explore the personal issues of home, house, and family with you.

Your Sun in Partner's Fifth House

You animate your partner's Fifth House of fun, play, pleasure, children, romance, and creativity. Not such bad homework here for the two of you—these are all activities born of the heart, with the intent of experiencing joy and creatively expressing yourselves. You can keep the spark of romance alive, as you will never tire of the courting and dating phase of your relationship. You also encourage confidence in your partner's creative expression.

Your Sun in Partner's Sixth House

You want to share in the day-to-day activities of your partner's life and wouldn't mind at all doing what you can to help your partner's life work more effectively—anything to help. It seems natural to tend to tasks and chores together, participate in health-conscious activities, and share many of the little things in life. Be careful not to overdo the role of advisor about what needs improving, or your partner may begin to wonder, "What is wrong with me the way that I am?"

Your Sun in Partner's Seventh House

This is one of the most favorable placements for relationships of all sorts. You bring out the very qualities that your partner most needs in relationships, plus this role feels natural to you. Issues that do arise have the best chance of being resolved, as you both are interested in each other's best interests. You value each other's feedback, favoring negotiations between the two of you.

Your Sun in Partner's Eighth House

Your Sun shines in your partner's Eighth House of deep secrets, so tread lightly until you are trusted. Once trusted, you have the capacity to open up what your partner has revealed to no other. You can be the perfect sexual partner who knows your lover's secret desires. Issues with shared resources and investments are favored. At times, you might be called to help your partner with issues around death. Yes, the Eighth House has it all: sex, death, and money. These are the most guarded aspects of anyone's character, and your Sun here shows the promise of establishing a truly transformative relationship, where you help each other take off the armor of past wounds, opening the door to intimacy.

Your Sun in Partner's Ninth House

You try to help expand your partner's perspective on life, and are a catalyst for your partner's interest in travel, education, philosophy, and the spiritual quest. Traveling together, even on long journeys, is favored with this placement. You animate each other's philosophical mind and can engage each other in the sport of debate in your search for truth. Principles and ethics are important with this placement. Finding a spiritual path that you both embrace is favored.

Your Sun in Partner's Tenth House

You are a strong support for your partner's ambitions to rise to the heights of what is possible in career and professional pursuits. You believe in your partner's potential and this belief gives him or her confidence. You don't want your partner's career to be separate from the relationship; your Sun in your partner's Tenth House shows this is an area in which you want to be actively involved. You like each other's public presentation and support each other's reputation.

Your Sun in Partner's Eleventh House

You empower the friendship connection in your relationship. This doesn't mean exclusively friendship—your relationship could include other dimensions as well—but the friendship is assured. This makes it easy to spend time together, hang out, and enjoy each other's company while taking part in social outings. Larger social issues can be important ways of sharing time together, as in volunteer work or social activism.

Your Sun in Partner's Twelfth House

You bring the light of your Sun into the most private part of your partner's life, what is going on behind the scenes, just beneath the surface. You can help your partner shed light on issues that have been unresolved from the past. This is ideal for relationships that include the spiritual quest, as you will strongly support your partner's spiritual life. Often, there seems to be something karmic about the relationship, as if there is some reason you are together. That feeling keeps you open to the mystic level of the Twelfth House and the hunger to know the meaning of what is going on in the event level of reality.

Moon in Each Other's Houses

The Moon represents the emotional side of your character and how you nurture yourself and others. Where it falls in your partner's chart is where you are comfortable in a supporting, nurturing role and where your emotional nature will have its strongest impact. Here is where you read your partner empathically, and feel, more than see, what is going on. It is also where you can have emotional reactions if you feel excluded in this area of your partner's life.

Your Moon in Partner's First House

You support your partner's self-identity by often deferring to his or her lead. You feel directly within yourself anything your partner is going through, making it almost impossible to separate your feelings from your partner's. Often found in family charts, this placement brings family issues into the relationship.

Your Moon in Partner's Second House

You nurture your partner's confidence in all matters of security. You help your partner feel that his or her skills, talents, and abilities are plenty adequate to lead to abundance. You will be emotionally impacted by any feelings of financial insecurity your partner may go through.

Your Moon in Partner's Third House

You nurture the day-to-day communications in the relationship. You like to stay informed, even about the little things. This can lead to many shared intellectual interests and pursuits. You are affected emotionally if your partner is not communicating with you or is withholding information; you thrive on the interaction.

Your Moon in Partner's Fourth House

You nurture the deepest feelings of home and family with your partner. You create a space for your partner to feel that it is safe to drop into his or her most natural way of being—like being at home. This placement is excellent for people who live together. You are emotionally affected if you feel excluded in your partner's need for retreat; you want that retreat to be with you.

Your Moon in Partner's Fifth House

You nurture the creative, playful aspect of the relationship. Romance comes easy; so do children! This is a fertile placement, not just for children, but for all activities of the heart. You support your partner's creative talents. Your feelings get hurt when your partner wants to have fun that doesn't include you.

Your Moon in Partner's Sixth House

You nurture your partner's day-to-day routines and like to find ways to be helpful. Even working together on mundane chores is all right with you. You like to tend to the little things that your partner can do to improve life. If you carry this too far, you can seem like the doting mother, or worse, the nag. Do what you can do to help your partner, and then learn to let things be.

Your Moon in Partner's Seventh House

This is one of the most favorable placements; you nurture the very qualities that your partner needs brought out in a relationship. You feel comfortable being the type of person your partner needs in a relationship. Your feelings get hurt if you are not included in important decisions in your partner's life. You want to be involved, particularly in all decisions that impact you.

Your Moon in Partner's Eighth House

You nurture a place within your partner that is normally kept secret from the world. The Eighth House of intimacy and shared resources is a private realm, but your Moon gives you access to these aspects of your partner's life and you are trusted with sensitivities rarely revealed to others. This can lead to a deeply meaningful tie, as it opens the door for emotional intimacy. You become emotionally affected if you feel your partner is keeping a secret from you.

Your Moon in Partner's Ninth House

You nurture the Ninth House of exploration for your partner. This exploration may be physical travel to faraway places, mental explorations through education, or philosophical explorations into religions and the spiritual quest. You nurture your partner's need to expand his or her view of life. You can feel emotionally put off if your partner offhandedly discredits a view of yours because it has an emotional base.

Your Moon in Partner's Tenth House

Your emotional nature impacts your partner's Tenth House of career, ambitions, and public standing. You align yourself as an emotional source of support for your partner in these areas and like to be a strength behind the scenes. You will also be emotionally impacted by the highs and lows of your partner's career and reputation.

Your Moon in Partner's Eleventh House

Your emotional nature impacts the friendship of this relationship. You seek to nurture what your partner needs in a friendship, leading to a strong emotional bond. You will support your partner's efforts in community service and all humanitarian endeavors. Your social horizons will be expanded through this relationship, and you can go through emotional reactions to some of your partner's friendships and ways of socializing, particularly when you are excluded.

Your Moon in Partner's Twelfth House

Your emotional patterns have a subconscious impact on your partner. There might be something inexplicable about your relationship, a tie that is not obvious to the world around. You can nurture your partner's need for quality time alone and spiritual pursuits. Things going on beneath the surface in your partner also impact you, things that she or he might not even be aware of. You both awaken deep emotional memories in each other, for good or ill.

Mercury in Each Other's Houses

Where your Mercury falls in your partner's chart is where you provide mental stimulation, and where the two of you can enjoy mutual intellectual interests. You like to talk about this area of your partner's life and bring new information to discuss. Communication is favored here and it is where you are going to want to be informed about matters concerning this area of your partner's life.

Your Mercury in Partner's First House

This placement is a confidence builder for both of you for expressing your ideas and acting on them. You are genuinely interested in your partner's views, and never tire of hearing the same stories. Your words have a strong impact on each other; at best, this inspires both of you, but of course words can wound as well. You encourage each other to speak up and be heard.

Your Mercury in Partner's Second House

With this placement, money matters can dominate the conversation. This is excellent for people working together to enhance each other's security and financial well-being. You provide your partner with ideas to further develop his or her skills, talents, and ability to enhance security. Your partner can stimulate you to think about the right use of resources—how to earn it and how to spend it.

Your Mercury in Partner's Third House

This is an excellent placement for all communication as you seek to bring ideas and gather information from your partner. The flow of conversation is enhanced by mutual intellectual interests; nothing seems too trivial. You spark each other's curiosity and naturally stay interested in all areas of each other's life, with a particular emphasis on staying informed of what is going on with each other's family.

Your Mercury in Partner's Fourth House

With this placement, your curiosity is focused on the most personal aspects of your partner's life. Matters concerning home, house, and family become topics of conversation. This is excellent for people living together who naturally want to talk about matters of the home, but for all people, this placement stimulates an interest in the most personal of issues. Taking time to be alone together enhances your communication with each other.

Your Mercury in Partner's Fifth House

You communicate in a way that stimulates your partner's sense of humor and playful attitude about life. This placement is favorable for shared interests in the fun things in life: recreation, entertainment, play, children, romance, and creativity. The playful quality of communication between the two of you enhances any relationship, but romance is particularly favored, as you will always have a knack for tickling your partner's heart.

Your Mercury in Partner's Sixth House

You are interested in the daily affairs of your partner's life, and this becomes a dominant arena of communication. This placement is excellent for people working together or carrying out the chores of everyday living. A mutual interest in health is indicated, and you bring information to each other to expand awareness on health issues. Proactively, this can lead to a mutual interest in pursuing information to support a healthy lifestyle. Reactively, it gives voice to each other's minor complaints of health problems.

Your Mercury in Partner's Seventh House

This is an excellent placement for any type of relationship, as you bring the information your partner needs to have a balanced perspective. It assures that you will both take each other's opinions into account when making joint decisions. This stimulates interest in the relationship itself, and you will find yourself discussing your relationship. A cooperative attitude is fostered, as you both are interested in what is fair for both of you. Shared intellectual endeavors are favored.

Your Mercury in Partner's Eighth House

This deep placement shows that you will be interested in your partner's secrets, things one's family wouldn't even know. This is excellent for intimate relationships and adds the mental component of curiosity to intimacy. You'll both want to be informed and considered in all issues concerning joint resources and investments. There can be mutual interest in the deep mysteries of life, the meaning of life and death, and a desire to know each other at the deepest level.

Your Mercury in Partner's Ninth House

This expansive placement puts your mental interests in your partner's Ninth House of all things foreign and ethnic, higher education, and philosophical, religious, and spiritual issues. Expect lively exchanges concerning political and worldly issues as well. The debate may be heated, but falls short of an argument, debate being the sport of the Ninth House. Discussions move up out of the purely personal and into the abstract world of ideas. This placement is ideal for students on any path together, as you both learn from each other and stimulate each other's interest in learning itself.

Your Mercury in Partner's Tenth House

You want to stay informed concerning your partner's career, so expect a great deal of discussion in this area of life. You can offer worthwhile perspectives on each other's role in the world, and can be valuable resources for each other in planning strategies for moving forward with your plans. This has a motivational impact on the relationship, as you both think about what you could achieve together.

Your Mercury in Partner's Eleventh House

You are interested in your partner's social world, and this placement assures a strong friendship connection between the two of you. You speak to each other as friends, no matter what your relationship is, and can enjoy social activities together. Your conversation can also drift toward dreams for the future. This placement can stimulate an interest in community service, larger social causes, political activism, and humanitarian endeavors.

Your Mercury in Partner's Twelfth House

This deep placement can show a mutual interest in each other's spiritual life and matters concerning consciousness growth. Your partner is drawn to discuss issues concerning dreams, mystical experiences, and private musings with you. Much communication beyond words exists between the two of you. The intuitive connection is very strong, and you will hear each other's unspoken words. This placement works best when you have a mutual interest in the spiritual side of life. Without this, the Twelfth House is most confusing, with miscommunications abounding.

Venus in Each Other's Houses

Venus placements are some of the most delightful in relationships. Where Venus falls in your partner's chart shows where you can enjoy mutual pleasure, appreciation of beauty, and some of the refinements in life. The Venus person seems like a lucky star here, attracting delightful people, situations, and resources into the partner's life.

Your Venus in Partner's First House

This placement enhances the physical magnetism between the two of you. This is obviously great for an amorous relationship, but there are many ways to pursue pleasure, beauty, and the arts. One way or another, you bring out each other's ability to enjoy life. Without some discipline, pleasure seeking could lead to indulgence, but with any refinement of character, you awaken in each other a great capacity to appreciate life.

Your Venus in Partner's Second House

Here, the magnetism of Venus can center on possessions and the material world. You awaken each other's appreciation for nice things. Shopping together can be fun. Sensory experiences are enhanced, and you bring out the connoisseur in each other, with mutual appreciation of fine dining, shopping, sunsets, and massages.

Your Venus in Partner's Third House

Here, you are attracted to your partner's mental pursuits, which creates a magnetic connection between your minds. You simply enjoy talking to each other. You will certainly find many things that you are both interested in learning. For example, you may share an interest in books, taking classes, or teaching classes. You can enjoy many intellectual pursuits together, with a leaning toward the arts. With this placement, it is not uncommon to get drawn into each other's extended family and siblings.

Your Venus in Partner's Fourth House

Here, your magnetism enhances the personal matters of house, home, and family for your partner. This placement is excellent for people living together, as just spending time together alone makes you both feel complete. You are most attracted to your partner when he or she drops all worldly efforts and just is. This allows you both to feel very natural around each other. You could enjoy beautifying a home together, spending family time, or finding beautiful places in nature to enjoy.

Your Venus in Partner's Fifth House

You are attracted to your partner's style of romance, and courting, dancing, and romancing can come from this connection. Knowing how to please each other comes naturally. This placement often reveals shared artistic interests, either as patrons or performers. Just going out and having fun together can be great. This placement also favors all mutual involvements with children.

Your Venus in Partner's Sixth House

Here, your magnetism is activated through sharing the daily activities and tasks of your partner. Working together in any setting can be very enjoyable; even simply helping each other tend to the details of life is made delightful with this combination. There can be a shared interest in health, working out together, or other shared fitness routines. Dining out at your favorite healthy restaurants would also be enjoyable.

Your Venus in Partner's Seventh House

This is one of the better placements of Venus for any relationship, but romantic relationships are especially enhanced. You are attracted to what your partner is looking for in a relationship, so it is a good match. You find each other enjoyable company no matter what the activity. This leads to a mutual appreciation for each other's feelings and considerations, and creates a friendly, affectionate relationship and a natural desire to please each other.

Your Venus in Partner's Eighth House

This is a very favorable placement for intimacy, and if other indicators support it, this is a wonderful placement for lovers. Your magnetism draws out the intimacy needs of your partner. Even if your relationship is not physical, you'll feel like it is safe to share intimate secrets with each other. Financial involvements together are favored, and you can even attract resources into the relationship from family or other sources.

Your Venus in Partner's Ninth House

You are attracted to your partner's higher mind, revealing a favorable philosophical rapport. You can enjoy each other's religious and political views, and find a similar spiritual path to share. An interest in higher education is shared, and encouraging each other to take classes and workshops to expand your worlds would be expected. Traveling together is favored, and even sharing dreams about potential travels to faraway places would be an enjoyable activity.

Your Venus in Partner's Tenth House

Here, the magnetism works to enhance each other's social standing, career, and ambitious pursuits. You are attracted to the way your partner carries himself or herself publicly. You bring out the best in each other's public presentation and enjoy each other's company at public outings. You may enjoy helping each other move toward career ambitions, and even attract a bit of luck in this regard.

Your Venus in Partner's Eleventh House

This placement brings magnetism to your friendship, leading to a rich social life together. You enjoy and value your partner's friendship, making it easy to spend time together, even if it is simply hanging out. Your tastes in friendships and socializing mix very well together, so you can enjoy socializing with other friends as well. Your social values are aligned, and you could find enjoyment in working for a common cause that you both believe in.

Your Venus in Partner's Twelfth House

Here, you are attracted to your partner's mystical and spiritual qualities. This can awaken what is going on behind the scenes, what is beneath the surface, and that which is not obvious to the outer world. This placement is best for a relationship that includes spiritual and consciousness growth. There is likely a feeling of something karmic and compelling about your relationship. If the spiritual side of life is not explored together, your partner can just seem weird, with Twilight Zone–type experiences. You can also pull each other down into indulgent habits if you don't work on developing consciousness.

Mars in Each Other's Houses

Mars is the forceful, dynamic, warrior planet and where it falls in each other's chart is an area that is heated up by this intensity. On the one hand, Mars is motivational, and where it falls in your partner's chart is where you can motivate your partner into action. You fortify your partner's courage here. On the other hand, this is where you can go too far and then Mars is just felt as pushy. You'll want to watch for signals from your partner in this area of life for when you have become pushy without even realizing it.

Your Mars in Partner's First House

This is a very energetic and dynamic placement for Mars. You motivate your partner into action, yet have to be careful not to be pushy and trigger defensiveness. A good release for the dynamic energy can be physical activity—sports, outdoor activity, even making love are all natural expressions of this energy. You give each other courage to push yourselves forward in life. If there is any tendency for physically striking out at each other in anger, you'd be advised to work on anger management and not let things get out of hand.

Your Mars in Partner's Second House

Here, the motivational energy of Mars impacts issues around money and finance. You can motivate your partner to gear up the earning potential to allow for more spending potential. Mars is potentially volatile and is always a hot spot in relationships. Here, you will both be prone to express hostilities around money and security-related issues. If you are aware of this tendency, then you can learn to be more mindful, and not let arguments over money have their full reign.

Your Mars in Partner's Third House

Mars motivates discussions in the Third House of communications. You want to know what your partner thinks about everything, and there may be times when your partner will feel badgered if you don't back off. This placement can be quite motivational for intellectual activities of all sorts. Discussions can become quite heated, leading to arguments if you try to change how each other thinks. Issues involving each other's siblings can be another volatile zone if not handled with some delicacy.

Your Mars in Partner's Fourth House

Here, your motivational energy enters into your partner's private arena of home, house, and family. This placement is great for doing projects together on the house or land, though it can make it difficult to relax together. With Mars being in the house of retreat, you come up with projects that need to be done for your retreat space. Conflict can erupt if either of you gets too bossy about projects you want the other person to do. Be careful of leaving "to do" lists for the other person to take care of while you are away. This has to be discussed tactfully, or it will trigger resentment. Issues concerning each other's family also have to be handled delicately to avoid hurting each other where you are most vulnerable.

Your Mars in Partner's Fifth House

You motivate your partner's Fifth House of creative expression. You can encourage each other to kick up your heels a little, have some fun, do something for the pure joy of it, get involved with children, and express yourself romantically or creatively. Fights can ensue if party hardy evolves into indulgence, or if you press your partner relentlessly for romance so that he or she feels pressured.

Your Mars in Partner's Sixth House

You demand action here in your partner's Sixth House of work, health, and daily routine. This is a very task-oriented placement, and you will need to find appropriate outlets for your energy, or the danger of becoming hypercritical of each other may arise. You two are at your best when you are focused on projects, such as work, tasks, chores, and the like. A strong focus on a shared fitness regime would be ideal for the Mars energy; otherwise, you feel like you are picking on each other.

Your Mars in Partner's Seventh House

Here, your warrior energy shows up in your partner's house of relationships. "If you can't take the heat, get out of the kitchen," applies here. Your relationship can be characterized as passionate, which is favorable in some arenas, yet very volatile in others. The pent-up energy of petty frustrations that Mars builds throughout the day gets released in the relationship. Disagreements can be passionate and too volatile for gentle souls. There is a fine line between being assertive and being abusive, and with this placement, you are advised to stay mindful of the line. You do help each other be more courageous in dealings with others, empowering each other to stand up for what's right and settle for nothing less.

Your Mars in Partner's Eighth House

Here, your motivational energy impacts the hidden world of your partner's Eighth House, for good or ill. This is ideal for a passionate, intimate relationship. For other types of relationships, this can be too close; your partner can feel overexposed. Because of the deep vulnerability that is bared, trust is essential; otherwise, your partner will feel you as being intrusive and shields will go up. This is an excellent placement for pursuing any type of research and investigative projects together. Mars here can be a two-edged sword around issues of investments. On the one hand, you give each other courage to make investments. But again, trust is essential; otherwise you run the risk of Mars battles being set off over mistrust issues, particularly with shared resources.

Your Mars in Partner's Ninth House

Here, your motivational energy activates your partner's principles, beliefs, and philosophical views about life. This is an excellent placement for students on any path of pursuing knowledge together; you motivate and prod each other to get stronger in your views. You will also challenge each other's beliefs. If you can handle this challenge so that the discussions stay at the level of debate and not argument, much clarity can develop. Travel can be a favorable outlet for this placement, particularly to faraway places and trips that include physical activity. You motivate each other to get out and explore and expand your horizons.

Your Mars in Partner's Tenth House

Your motivational energy impacts your partner's ambitions to succeed. You can motivate each other to reach for the heights of what is possible and would defend each other's reputation if it ever came to that. If you are united in your goals, you will accomplish much together. If your ambitions are not aligned with each other, your pushy nature could be felt by your partner as badgering around career issues.

Your Mars in Partner's Eleventh House

With this placement, your motivational energy heats up your partner's Eleventh House of friendships and social causes. This brings some volatility to your friendship and works best when you dedicate this intensity to social causes you both support. When you get pushy, your partner feels pressured into taking part in some unwanted social activity. Issues with each other's friends, and how each of you socializes, can be triggers for conflict.

Your Mars in Partner's Twelfth House

This is another tricky placement for Mars. You heat up the hidden material in your partner's consciousness. Mars activates this hidden side of life and, at best, is highly motivational for spiritual pursuits. Deep trust is a requirement for the relationship to progress; otherwise, the mistrust over each other's motivations would limit closeness. Taking part in some spiritual activity together involving physical movement, like yoga or tai chi, would be ideal. You may violate your partner's need for quality alone time if you don't read the clues.

Jupiter in Each Other's Houses

Where your Jupiter falls in each other's chart is where you want to be generous with each other and help expand each other's horizons. Being the largest planet, Jupiter shows where you want to do things on a grand scale. It is where you can encourage each other to take a more philosophical, positive, and expansive view of life. It is also where you can be too generous; Jupiter has a way of exploiting excessive tendencies, and this area of life is where you can be vulnerable to "too-much-itis."

Your Jupiter in Partner's First House

This placement encourages a positive, "let's take a big bite out of life" attitude for both individuals. You look out for your partner's best interests, and this promotes trust. You inspire and give confidence to each other to reach for the fullness that life has to offer. Travel, outdoor activities, and philosophical studies are particularly favored.

Your Jupiter in Partner's Second House

Here, the expansive qualities of Jupiter impact financial and security-related themes. You inspire your partner's confidence in his or her earning capacity, and it is not uncommon for you to want to be a benefactor to help your partner financially. This placement leads to mutual enjoyment of the material world and its bounty, and there can be a bit of luck with joint money issues. The excessive tendencies of Jupiter have to curbed, or overspending can lead to debt problems.

Your Jupiter in Partner's Third House

Here, your expansive qualities impact your partner's communication and mental interests. You won't get bored with each other—there will always be opportunities for learning and discussion between the two of you. This heightens the mental curiosity and interest in education in both of you. You will likely have ongoing discussions with each other in your minds, even when you are not together. Philosophy, religion, and politics are favorite Jupiter topics, but all learning is enhanced with this placement. Short travels, particularly to connect with each other's siblings and extended family, often come with this placement.

Your Jupiter in Partner's Fourth House

Here, you seek to improve conditions for your partner's issues with home, house, and family. This placement enhances personal time together, with deep discussions about the most personal issues. It can be very rewarding to be alone together, away from the world. For people living together, this helps create a positive attitude in family dynamics and a drive to constantly improve your house to make it a more nurturing environment. Jupiter likes space and big places, which is all well and good, but you'll have to watch out for the tendency to always want your house to be just a little bit bigger and better.

Your Jupiter in Partner's Fifth House

Here, you seek to expand all matters of the heart, fun, romance, children, and creativity for your partner. This is a very fertile placement and encourages the attitude of "Why not enjoy life?" This placement extends the romance years long beyond the courting phase of your relationship, as you enjoy bringing out the heartfelt, celebratory qualities of life in each other. You inspire confidence in your partner's attitude toward creative endeavors. Problems with Jupiter's excessiveness can show up if either of you has difficulties with drugs, alcohol, or gambling.

Your Jupiter in Partner's Sixth House

You want to help your partner's life run more smoothly by contributing in little ways. This is a project placement, and the two of you encourage each other to get more done in the course of the day. Your partner wants to help you find effective, step-by-step ways of achieving your goals. A mutual interest in each other's health can be present, and taking part in a diet and fitness program together can be rewarding. You encourage each other to seek the training you need to improve your skills and talents. A tendency to cram too many things into a day needs to be curbed, or you will feel overwhelmed by the sheer number of positive activities Jupiter presents.

Your Jupiter in Partner's Seventh House

You seek to expand and improve your partner's experience of relationships. All cooperative involvements are made more enjoyable with this placement, and there is a strong sense of possibility of what you can do together. You feel more confident in making important decisions after receiving each other's counsel because of the strong trust between you. This also expands the number of people who want to get involved with the two of you, and if you are not mindful, your lives can become too caught up in all the people in your life.

Your Jupiter in Partner's Eighth House

Here, your expansive qualities work behind the scenes in your partner's private Eighth House, which promotes trust in revealing secrets to each other. This is an excellent placement for lovers and promotes intimacy, because of the trust. This trust also favors shared resources and investments, but you will have to be mindful of Jupiter's tendency to be overly optimistic. When this is the case, you can encourage each other into debt! Deep subjects like psychology, the occult, the meaning of death, and anything a bit mysterious are favored intellectual pursuits.

Your Jupiter in Partner's Ninth House

This is Jupiter's natural house and it is free to do what it does best here: inspire you both to take a more expansive approach to life. You bring out the adventurer in each other; travel and involvement with all things foreign and ethnic are favored activities. Supporting and taking part in each other's spiritual quest is also favored. The low road of Jupiter here leads to dogmatic arguments and proselytizing. To take advantage of this placement, work on expanding your own beliefs by exploring the world's religions and philosophical teachings.

Your Jupiter in Partner's Tenth House

Here, your expansive qualities seek to benefit your partner's career ambitions and social standing. You want to be benefactors for helping each other get ahead in life. You promote each other and encourage each other to take a positive view about reaching your aspirations. Jupiter's problem of too much of a good thing can lead to the "victim of success" syndrome, where your relationship suffers because of all the worldly success you generate together.

Your Jupiter in Partner's Eleventh House

This placement leads to an enjoyable friendship for the two of you. You seek to expand your partner's social horizons. You will likely have many mutual friends, and the prospects for finding social activities that you both enjoy are greatly enhanced. Group activities and social causes that you both believe in are favored Eleventh House activities. When out of hand, Jupiter can lead to an excessive focus on "the cause" *du jour,* squeezing out needs for the personal side of the relationship.

Your Jupiter in Partner's Twelfth House

This placement promotes spiritual growth for both of you. The Twelfth House is where we retreat from life's activities to contemplate the deeper meaning of it all. You encourage this deeper searching in your partner, often leading to shared interests in the mystical aspects of life. Dreams, meditation, and spiritual explorations are favored activities to explore together. Compassion is born out of this, compassion for each other and for the world, leading to a desire to be of service to those in need. You want to help each other in unseen ways, like being guardian angels for each other. The excessive problems associated with Jupiter could manifest if either of you has escapist tendencies with drugs or alcohol.

Saturn in Each Other's Houses

Where your Saturn fits in each other's chart will be experienced as a two-edged sword. On the one hand, its house placement can be an area where you make commitments to each other and build something of significance. Saturn demands self-control, hard work, and perseverance, and these qualities pay off where Saturn shows up in each other's chart. It is also where challenges will show up. Saturn reveals problems; it doesn't create them, but it does reveal them. So where Saturn shows up is where you must realistically face the issues that arise. Saturn presents the tough lessons in life and, in truth, only the strong survive.

The best relationships get stronger from facing and dealing with the challenges that Saturn reveals. The weak relationships crash and burn in the Saturn house. This statement is a bit overly dramatic to be sure, but Saturn is that important. Show up for the work it demands and your relationship will get stronger; try to dodge Saturn issues and you sign up for a world of difficulties.

Your Saturn in Partner's First House

Here, you are a molding and structuring influence on your partner's confidence in self-expression. The two sides of Saturn's sword in your partner's First House lead to either a strong commitment to each other based on loyalty, or a relationship that can feel like an oppressive responsibility. Respect is the key difference. With respect, you grow stronger by being with someone who sees your weaknesses and gives you the strength of character to work through them. You know you have someone in your corner through thick and thin. Without respect, you see each other's weaknesses, but with no desire to help, you can pull each other down.

Your Saturn in Partner's Second House

You seek to curb and restrain your partner's spending impulses, but if not handled wisely, your partner can feel diminished confidence and a lack of security from the fear of disapproval. When handled at its best, this placement leads to slow steady growth in financial security for the relationship. Saturn encourages obtaining wealth the old-fashioned way: you earn it through hard work, cautious and wise investments, and paying attention to what to not spend money on—these are the attitudes that will pay off for the two of you financially. The low road would lead to your partner feeling you to be a financial burden, although it is not uncommon that the responsibility is appropriate and not a burden at all, as with children.

Your Saturn in Partner's Third House

You promote a serious, disciplined approach to learning and communication for your partner. This is the ideal placement for serious students, researchers, educators, writers, and the like. You bring out a professional, scholarly approach to your partner's intellectual pursuits, not that it will always be smooth in this regard. Your keen eye reveals weaknesses in the mental pursuits and communication of your partner. Communication over mutual projects goes well enough, but casual conversation feels strained. If not handled proactively, this can lead to negative patterns of criticizing each other's thoughts and ideas, or having conversations that only focus on current difficulties.

Your Saturn in Partner's Fourth House

You are a structuring influence on your partner's highly personal issues of home, house, and family. Saturn is not warm and cozy here, but can give you the strength of commitment that it takes to maintain a home together. You get pulled into each other's family issues, for good or ill. Projects and chores around the house and land are perfect, including actually building a house together. When mutual respect is present, you count on each other for authoritative guidance concerning personal matters. The low road of Saturn would lead your partner to feel burdened by your lifestyle or demands of how to keep a home. If there is inflexibility here, living together would be difficult.

Your Saturn in Partner's Fifth House

The restraining influence of Saturn is not thought to be favorable when placed in your partner's Fifth House of the heart and romance, but if it's the right relationship, there can be a strong commitment based on the romance. Saturn's restricting influence doesn't necessarily block your partner's creative expression, but it does encourage more perspiration than inspiration to bring creativity into manifestation. If handled wisely, you can share responsibility for raising children together with all the perseverance and commitment this requires. The low road of Saturn here leads to difficulties with each other's style of parenting. Also, your partner can feel as if you limit all opportunities for fun and creative expression.

Your Saturn in Partner's Sixth House

Here, Saturn applies its pressure in your partner's Sixth House of work, health, and daily routines. The ideal would be for you to be a mentor for your partner in some way. It is appropriate for a mentor to see what the student needs for self-improvement, so this arrangement works. It is all too easy for your partner to feel picked on if you are relentless with critical feedback. How this information is delivered makes all the difference. Pointing out the flaws has a different impact than demonstrating a better way to do something. This placement could be good for working together if, and only if, you restrain the impulse to manage every detail of your partner's life.

Your Saturn in Partner's Seventh House

You are a molding influence for what your partner is looking for in a relationship. If you both are committed to the same ideal in the relationship, this creates a lasting strength that allows you to make it through the tough times. With this placement, you will reveal the flaws in the relationship, and only the best will survive. It takes skill to process the difficulties that naturally arise in a relationship. If issues are not processed when they arise, they accumulate, leading to a storehouse of resentments. The low road leads to an uncomfortable fit in the relationship. Your standards of what you are looking for in a relationship could be disappointing to each other and difficulties may arise over whose responsibility is whose.

Your Saturn in Partner's Eighth House

You are a molding and restricting influence on your partner's issues with intimacy and shared resources. Saturn is tricky enough to deal with in any relationship, but with the pressures of Saturn here, you are advised to stay mindful of its possible downfalls—to avoid them is the goal. You must remain impeccable in all of your dealings with each other to avoid issues of mistrust. With trust, you can handle the responsibilities of shared resources together, and make wise, cautious investments. You can assist each other in fulfilling responsibilities concerning death, should you be faced with such a dire necessity. With the low road there are issues of mistrust to deal with. Intimacy can lack tenderness and your partner can feel pressured for sex as if it were a duty, unless you compensate for the business-like ways of Saturn. Arguments can erupt over how the two of you handle money. Again, impeccability with all issues concerning shared resources is what Saturn demands, and is the path to take to avoid the pitfalls of this placement.

Your Saturn in Partner's Ninth House

Here, your molding influence makes an impact on your partner's Ninth House of higher education, philosophy, religion, and political views. This leads to a relationship where you both take these issues seriously. This placement is ideal for scholars who together are trying to hone their knowledge into a working belief system that meshes with the world. At best, you take the abstract material of your partner and forge a grounded, realistic philosophy. Traveling together, just for the fun of it, is not favored, but traveling for educational or professional reasons is strongly supported. The low road would lead to your partner feeling pressured to conform to your beliefs.

Your Saturn in Partner's Tenth House

Saturn is potentially at its best in your partner's Tenth House, the house that it naturally rules. Here, you are a molding and structuring influence on your partner's career and ambitions. This is a particularly favorable placement for a relationship between two people with shared career interests—you definitely can benefit from each other's counsel concerning matters of getting ahead in the world. Saturn brings pressure, not just support, and reveals the slow, steady, determined path to success. If you get defensive of each other's opinions around career, you will miss valuable information that could be gained concerning where you could improve. Of course, how you share the information you hold from the Saturn perspective makes all the difference in the world; at best, you are a mentor to your partner; at worst, a repressive tyrant.

Your Saturn in Partner's Eleventh House

You are a molding and restricting influence on your partner's social life and friendships. Your serious nature colors the nature of your friendship with your partner. You're not comfortable just hanging out together, but prefer to have projects, and with the Eleventh House, these projects would lean toward service groups, organizations, and social causes. Your friendship works best when you are involved in mutual projects and commitments to these larger social concerns. However, there are likely to be certain social interests that you do not share well, and how you handle these will be important. Will you honor your different social needs and give each other support to pursue separate interests? Or will you be restrictive in each other's social life, holding each other back?

Your Saturn in Partner's Twelfth House

You are a molding and restricting influence on your partner's spiritual interests. This is best for relationships with a shared commitment to a spiritual path, and since Saturn encourages discipline, having a shared spiritual practice would be ideal. To experience the best of this placement, at a minimum there has to be honor and respect for each other's spiritual beliefs, even if they are not the same. Without this mutual respect, you will not feel safe sharing the deepest you, and much of the relationship will go unexplored. At worst, you could pull each other down into old karmic patterns.

Uranus in Each Other's Houses

Uranus is the first of the outer planets, which all deal with forces beyond the ego. Where it falls in each other's chart is where you will encourage each other to cast off cultural convention to discover your authentic nature. It is also an area where each other's independence can be perceived as threatening to the needs of the relationship.

Your Uranus in Partner's First House

You have a liberating effect on your partner's personality. You feel more uninhibited than usual in each other's presence, and this liberates the personality for self-expression. You encourage each other to act out of character and try things that normally would be rejected. If either of you is already so unconventional that you have trouble fitting in to society anyway, this relationship only accentuates your difficulties. But if either of you has been bound by convention or other people's expectations, this relationship can help set you free.

Your Uranus in Partner's Second House

You have a liberating effect on your partner's financial security needs. You encourage each other to be innovative in the skills you develop to provide for yourselves. Uranus encourages a "wheel of fortune" attitude about financial issues. This radical attitude about money most often leads to dramatic changes in the financial stability of the relationship, for good or ill. Your relationship looks at money as energy rather than something to possess, so you tend to keep the money moving rather than finding security in saving it.

Your Uranus in Partner's Third House

You have a liberating effect on your partner's Third House of communication. This is an excellent placement for encouraging each other to explore new intellectual frontiers. You challenge each other to speak your personal truth, regardless of whether it is socially acceptable or not. This placement liberates original thinking for both of you, because you will challenge each other to go beyond conventional thinking. Unexpected behavior from either of your siblings or extended family can enter into your conversations.

Your Uranus in Partner's Fourth House

You have a liberating effect on your partner's Fourth House issues of home and family. You will encourage each other to break free of issues concerning your family of origin to discover your authentic needs for creating your own home and family. You could become interested in alternative lifestyles, like alternative housing, or at least create a highly original home together. Some with this placement will act on their independent urge and move toward a self-sufficient lifestyle.

Your Uranus in Partner's Fifth House

You have a liberating effect on your partner's creative expression. You could encourage each other to break free from convention to be more innovative in creative endeavors. There could be something unique about your romance together, as Uranus has no interest in fitting into expected patterns. If there are children in the relationship, you will encourage each other to break free of conventional attitudes, and, since Uranus has no interest in control, you would support each other in allowing freedom of expression in children.

Your Uranus in Partner's Sixth House

You have a liberating effect your partner's attitudes about work, health, and daily routines. The Sixth House is where we need mentors to acquire training to improve skills we're interested in developing, particularly those related to work. Uranus can be disruptive in this regard, because this placement encourages both of you to break from tradition and strike out on your own. This is excellent for those with entrepreneurial leanings. You will also encourage each other to break from the cultural attitude about health care to discover a program that is uniquely suited to your needs.

Your Uranus in Partner's Seventh House

You have a liberating effect on your partner's attitudes about relationships. Uranus doesn't like to play by the rules of the culture, so expect there to be something unusual about your relationship. It may have a decidedly mental flavor, with both of you encouraging each other to stay on the cutting edge of personal discovery within the relationship. Uranus is destabilizing; it forces the relationship to constantly evolve and become a vehicle for each other's awakening,

Your Uranus in Partner's Eighth House

You have a liberating effect on your partner's attitudes concerning sexuality and shared resources. This encourages an innovative, experimental approach to your intimacy together. You might find that your intimacy cycle with each other is interrupted by periods when you both need space for your individuality. You encourage each other to think outside of the box with investments, but the unpredictable nature of Uranus leads this to be a "wheel of fortune" placement for shared resources—some of your ideas together could be golden and some could "go bust." You could have experiences around death together that force you both to evolve.

Your Uranus in Partner's Ninth House

You have a liberating effect on your partner's philosophical beliefs. You encourage each other to throw off conventional attitudes concerning higher education, religion, and politics, challenging each other to evolve to a liberated worldview. You encourage each other to honor your radical individuality as the source for knowing truth. Politically, you encourage the social activist in each other with interest in reforming laws that restrict individual rights.

Your Uranus in Partner's Tenth House

You have a liberating effect on your partner's career ambitions. You encourage each other to other to break from the pack, ignore public opinion, and pursue a career that is unique. You encourage each other to stay on the path of discovery with your career, rather than just carry on with routine. Uranus places no stock in public opinion, and this placement unchecked could have an adverse impact on your public reputation together.

Your Uranus in Partner's Eleventh House

You have a liberating effect on your partner's social interests. Uranus is the natural ruler of the Eleventh House, and thus free to do what it does best: liberate each other to consider alternative lifestyles. You encourage each other to explore alternative routes into the culture, and the people you meet on this path of discovery will open you to further explorations. You attract interesting friends together as you are open to original thinkers and social activists. The two of you may become interested in movements aimed at social reform. Friendships that are influenced by Uranus are typically electric and unpredictable rather than warm and cozy.

Your Uranus in Partner's Twelfth House

You have a liberating effect on your partner's deep psyche and restricting memories. With training in meditation and exploring other states of consciousness, this can lead to a highly intuitive, nearly telepathic rapport. Your influence frees your partner from restricting memories of past events. You can encourage each other to pursue a spiritual path that is authentically suited for you, regardless of the beliefs of others, leading to shared interests in many mystical and magical studies. For people who have not pursued an understanding of the inner world, this connection can just seem weird.

Neptune in Each Other's Houses

Neptune, another of the outer planets, takes us far beyond the realms of the ego's understanding. It represents the urge for transcendence. Neptune functions as the imagination, which leads to both inspiration and the blind spot of illusion—seeing things how you want them to be rather than how they really are. This can lead to a mystical and magical connection when inspired, and to the despair of broken dreams when based on delusion. These are the issues to watch for where Neptune is in each other's chart.

Your Neptune in Partner's First House

You can either inspire your partner toward spiritual and artistic ideals, or delude him or her into a blind spot. This is a wonderful placement for artists and spiritual seekers; with these paths you can trust you are aiming at the best of Neptune. With the low road, you might not be seeing each other for who you really are, or you could lead each other into escapist behavior of one type or another.

Your Neptune in Partner's Second House

Here, your inspirational, or delusional, qualities impact your partner's Second House of security and financial issues. The range of influence is tremendous; from inspiring each other toward lofty ideals about money, such as conscious spending or donating a portion of one's earnings toward humanitarian causes, to deluding each other into making the poorest choices imaginable concerning money. A good rule of thumb for the two of you with regard to all major purchases is to get advice first; Neptune's blind spot is lurking. The financial difficulties that could come from a misguided Neptune, imagining all types of potential that doesn't exist, could be disastrous.

Your Neptune in Partner's Third House

Your imagination influences your partner's mind, and your conversations can soar beyond the commonplace. Writers, poets, and romantics would love this placement. Spiritual and artistic topics lead to inspired conversations. Although conversations about the mystical are inspiring, day-to-day communications can be mystifying, with both of you feeling like you understood your communication together, yet you understood it in two different ways.

Your Neptune in Partner's Fourth House

Your subtle influence will either be a source of inspiration or confusion for your partner's need to create strong foundations. Here, the inspirational impact of Neptune can lead the two of you to find sanctuary in nature as spiritually rejuvenating. This same sacred awareness can be brought into the home, and the two of you benefit with reclusive time together for meditation, music, poetry, reading, and watching movies at home. When Neptune is not well managed, it can erode your attempts to live together and carry out the responsibilities of managing the affairs of a home.

Your Neptune in Partner's Fifth House

Your imaginative qualities influence your partner's Fifth House of creative self-expression, inspiring a wide range of creative potential in the relationship. This placement can bring imaginative play into your romance. The low road could lead to infatuation with each other, falling in love with that which isn't real. The worst-case scenario for those who are undisciplined with imagination is debauchery, indulgences, and poor choices with speculation and gambling. But the best of Neptune brings vision and inspiration into the romance and all involvements of the heart, including children.

Your Neptune in Partner's Sixth House

To bring out the best of this placement, your inspired energy needs to be integrated into the daily affairs of your partner. Encouraging each other toward the humble path of work as spiritual service is the high road, but this is not a great combination for actually working together; you are on two different channels as far as the right way to go about completing tasks. The low road is mostly distracting. Instead of helping each other's life work more smoothly, you can distract each other from following through with the details of everyday living. Another possible blind spot would be encouraging false optimism in each other's health to the point that you both neglect it.

Your Neptune in Partner's Seventh House

This placement brings your inspiration, or delusions, right into the relationship itself for your partner. You can develop shared interests in the mystical, spiritual aspects of life and become aware of your subtle energy bodies and their interaction through your relationship. You can develop a strong psychic link and certainly need to pay as much attention to your unspoken words as your spoken words. The downside of this placement starts off innocently enough: you see each other's potential at the soul level, but not the here-and-now actual reality. The prospect of falling in love with false images of what is truly possible in the relationship runs strong. Another low road is avoidance, which also starts off innocently—you two have the ability to transcend the little things. This is all fine until you start avoiding major issues, and then trouble sets in from a growing accumulation of unresolved issues.

Your Neptune in Partner's Eighth House

This placement brings your imaginative and sensitive qualities into your partner's Eighth House of intimacy. This is a deep and mystical connection for those skilled with handling imagination. Explorations into the occult, deep psychology, and a spiritual understanding of death are all favored. Incorporating imagination into lovemaking can lead to sacred sexuality, or eroticism, or both. At worst, there could be deceptions around intimacy and financial dealing with each other. If you get funny feelings about any financial dealings that you have together, work it out before you proceed and you'll avoid the agony that comes from Neptune's blind spot.

Your Neptune in Partner's Ninth House

Here, your inspirational qualities can soar in your partner's Ninth House of the higher mind. This placement inspires mutual interest in the mystical side of spirituality and religion. You can find a shared interest in a spiritual path, a teaching, or a guru. If Neptune is undisciplined, you can be led by illusions in your search for truth. Remember that the true teachings bring you home to your own still, quiet voice within, and a rapport with the Divine. False teachings and teachers lead you into the teachings, or the teacher, rather than yourself.

Your Neptune in Partner's Tenth House

Your imagination influences your partner's career and standing in the community. You inspire each other to reach beyond traditional careers and to pursue ambitions involving creativity or compassion. When Neptune's blind spot is active, you imagine business potential that just isn't there. This shouldn't be underestimated with this combination, and you should ask yourselves, "Have we examined every scenario of any business venture we are considering?" Knowing Neptune's blind spot with this placement, it would be wise to at least consider what would happen if your plans don't work. Then you can't be blindsided.

Your Neptune in Partner's Eleventh House

You can either be inspiring or confusing for your partner's friendship issues. At best, you enjoy social activities together that inspire both of you; the arts, music, dance, and groups that explore mysticism and meditation are favored. You inspire altruism in each other, and you want to reach out to your culture with compassion. At another level, you promote each other's social activities that are purely escapist in nature, like the bar scene or whatever fantasyland attracts the two of you. The low road would be to engage in gossip, or even slander, about each other with other friends.

Your Neptune in Partner's Twelfth House

Your imagination and sensitivity impact your partner's inner, spiritual life. Neptune is operating in its natural house here, and thus you have strong potential to manifest the best and worst of its influence. This placement enhances the psychic, intuitive link between the two of you; you might even be in each other's dreams. For the spiritually inclined, this can lead to shared mystical experiences that strengthen your faith in a world beyond the senses. For those not skilled with Neptune, this placement enhances fears, illusions, escapist tendencies, and the like. Drugs and alcohol usually enhance the distortions of reality that are the problem in the first place.

Pluto in Each Other's Houses

Pluto is the farthest planet away from the Sun, and brings forces to bear on a situation that are the furthest away from the center of your conscious identity. In relationships, Pluto brings powerful, subconscious forces into play in each other's life. It is either where deep transformation will occur from helping each other to become more conscious, or where power issues can erupt, fueled by forces neither of you are aware of. It is precisely where you can help each other become conscious of previously subconscious motivations. This is touchy material. Here is where you see each other's idiosyncrasies and subconscious behavior patterns.

Where Pluto falls in each other's chart is where there can be power and control games going on between the two of you that you seemingly can't break out of. If you can step outside of these control issues, there can be tremendous growth in consciousness for both of you, fueled by the passion of aligning with your soul's purpose.

Your Pluto in Partner's First House

Here, your transformational energy impacts your partner's self-identity and self-expression. The molding influence of Pluto can be felt as intimidating or empowering. It is important for your partner to believe that you are acting with great integrity, or defensive alarms will go off. Power struggles and control games erupt over your partner's need for independent action.

Your Pluto in Partner's Second House

You bring about transformational changes in your partner's issues with money, possessions, and financial well-being. The best of this placement helps you both dig deeper into your souls to find core skills, talents, and abilities that you were meant to draw on to provide for your security and abundance. This can bring out a passion for money, for good or ill. With the high road, you can help each other align with the right distribution of wealth—the more you allow to come to you, the more you have to distribute to the causes and needs you believe in. The low road fuels a neurotic hunger for security, which is insatiable at the material level. You unconsciously seek to control your partner's financial issues, for good or ill. (Again, remember that astrology just reveals energy patterns; your choice of how to handle the energy is free will.)

Your Pluto in Partner's Third House

This is one of the better placements for deep transformational communication between the two of you. You drive your partner to dig deeper into mental pursuits. Research or studying together would be ideal for putting the x-ray energy of Pluto to worthy application. You can also help each other become conscious of unconscious speech patterns. Control issues can erupt if your partner has thoughts and views that are not in alignment with your own.

Your Pluto in Partner's Fourth House

You have a transformational impact on your partner's deepest identity formed in early family life. This material is largely subconscious in us anyway, and this is precisely the material that Pluto will bring up to be transformed. You can help each other become conscious of these molding influences of family, so that you can transform them and create a home and family that is more appropriate for your soul needs. Control issues can erupt if you seek to control your partner in matters concerning the home. If you can't relax your will when the two of you are home together, your partner will have difficulty experiencing the feeling of sanctuary that is necessary.

Your Pluto in Partner's Fifth House

This placement takes the normally playful aspect of sexuality in romance and transforms it with passion. You seek to unlock the mystery of your partner's pleasure. On the low road, there could be obsessive behavior in this regard. You can awaken deep creative fires in your partner, and a passionate involvement in the arts or other arenas of creative self-expression can be great for your relationship. It is often the case that destiny brings your lives together through children. If either of you is vulnerable to indulgences or gambling, caution must be advised with this placement.

Your Pluto in Partner's Sixth House

Your transformational energy impacts your partner's Sixth House of work and health. The Sixth House is also where we deal with unequal relationships of all kinds, like employer-employee, which is unequal by definition. Pluto here can accentuate this inequality, and the worst-case scenario manifests as a dominant-submissive relationship. At best, you assist your partner in perfecting a skill with the kind eyes of a mentor. If excessive, your partner can feel oppressed by your relentless nagging. Destiny brings issues around service, health, and healing into the relationship.

Your Pluto in Partner's Seventh House

You bring transformational energy into the relationship itself for your partner—neither of you will walk away from this relationship unscathed! At best, you form a passionate bond that helps you both purge that which had been standing in the way of this deepest type of commitment. There can be something karmic about the relationship in that you seem to have to overcome some difficulties that the two of you have to face, a karmic make-it-or-break-it test that, once passed, leads to a depth of commitment beyond contract. If the Pluto person can't see his or her tendency to control the direction of the relationship, there can be power and control issues erupting, making it difficult to make even the simplest of agreements. If you can forge your two wills together as one, your combined energy is unstoppable.

Your Pluto in Partner's Eighth House

This is Pluto's natural house and will bring out its strongest influence. There can be something compelling about your relationship. At best, you can bring about deep sexual and intimate healing for your partner. The Pluto passion, to go deeper, can lead to the psychological dimension of sexuality with interests in eroticism and tantra. Relationships that are not sexual often lead to an interest in the psychological, mystical, and occult aspects of life. You could be called on to help each other through life's profound tests, like death. The Pluto person will tend to control joint resources, which is perfect if by cooperative arrangement, but not so perfect if it isn't. Power and control issues could erupt over the handling of joint resources and issues around sexuality. You unknowingly awaken the wounds of intimacy that your partner has stored as armor. Your relationship will take passage through this territory, and if you survive this as a couple, great transformational healing will take place.

Your Pluto in Partner's Ninth House

Here, the theater of the higher mind of your partner becomes the cauldron for your transformative power. You seek to transform and deepen your partner's beliefs. There can be a deep interest in sharing the passion of a spiritual path together. The high road leads to a deepening of each other's beliefs by pouring into particular teachings that you are drawn to. Sometimes the destiny is revealed through travel and involvements with all that is foreign and ethnic, particularly religions. In all ways, the soul's purpose is going to be revealed through helping each other move beyond biases, prejudices, and narrow thinking to allow your spirits to soar into a larger view of possibility. You may have control issues over education, religion, and politics.

Your Pluto in Partner's Tenth House

Here, your transformative power impacts your partner's issues around career and social standing. Destiny may weave your two lives together through becoming inextricably involved with each other's career. The coming together of your relationship may cause a disruption in your social standing and reputation. Control issues can erupt if you seek too much control and dominance over your partner's life direction.

Your Pluto in Partner's Eleventh House

Here, your transformative power impacts the friendship level of the relationship for your partner. This placement puts your friendship to the test with periodic upheavals, as Pluto brings subconscious issues to the forefront. Ideally, Pluto helps you both purge control/surrender tendencies you have in friendships. This clears the way for the rejuvenation phase of your friendship. Pluto's tendency here is to push the friendship beyond mere hanging out, and to bring a greater depth. Your friendship will include confrontations with the shadow side of each other, and how you deal with this makes all the difference. Can you accept the shadow truth about each other and still grow in friendship? Or will revelations of each other's shadows intimidate you to the point of closing off from the friendship altogether? The soul's purpose of the relationship could also be revealed through a compelling interest that you share for altruistic causes.

Your Pluto in Partner's Twelfth House

The best of this placement is brought out when there is a shared interest in the spiritual, mystical aspects of life. You activate your partner's issues concerning all that is going on beneath the surface in the hidden inner world. There are compelling issues about your relationship that others will never see. At best, you help each other transform the sub-conscious material of repressed past experiences into the conscious awareness of lessons your soul has been revealing to you. At worst, you activate the karmic patterns that pull the relationship down and into self-sabotaging behavior patterns. This placement is best for relationships where the two of you actively support each other's soul growth.

The Nodes in Each Other's Houses

The nodal axis is made up of the North Node and the South Node, which are always exactly opposite each other. This is your "axis of incarnation." The South Node represents the inherited skills, talents, and abilities that you brought with you from your own past lives. It is the path of least resistance, because of its familiarity, and it is where you have much to give, but it is not an area of growth—you've already been cast in that role. The North Node is where you will find food for soul growth in this life. Although growth-oriented, it is not familiar, and thus not comfortable. Growth here needs to be allowed, more than sought after. Where your North Node falls in your partner's chart shows the area where your partner's life is a good role model for your personal soul growth. The house where your South Node falls in your partner's chart is familiar territory for your soul—you have much to give here, but not as much to gain.

Your North Node in Partner's First House/South Node in Seventh House

You have something to learn about promoting the self from the natural expression of your partner. The path of soul growth for the relationship includes promoting each other's separate ability to make independent choices. The path of least resistance is when one of you excessively defers to the other in important decisions; as in waiting to make sure the choice you are about to make is approved by your partner before you act. Your default setting is to consider each other when making important decisions; you don't have to worry about that. Your growth comes in being able to make independent choices based on your own instincts.

Your North Node in Partner's Second House/South Node in Eighth House

Your path of soul growth is entwined with your partner's financial security needs. The path of least resistance with this placement leads to getting so involved in your partner's resources that you forget to develop your own. You instinctively know the way to each other's passions (South Node in the Eighth House), but soul growth comes by making your love more comfortable and less desperate.

Your North Node in Partner's Third House/South Node in Ninth House

Your path of soul growth is aligned with your partner's natural way of learning and communicating. This opens up a great deal of territory as growth comes from encouraging each other to stay open-minded to learning opportunities. The path of least resistance is to encourage any type of high-mindedness, or prejudice, in each other.

Your North Node in Partner's Fourth House/South Node in Tenth House

The path that will nurture your soul will come through sharing the most personal aspects of life with your partner. The way your partner naturally relates to issues of home, house, and family, and even nature, is food for your soul growth. All issues that would stem from living together—projects connected to the house and land, involvements with family, and the personal side of life—are growth-oriented. The path of least resistance is to get so caught up in career and ambitious pursuits that you don't have any quality personal time together.

Your North Node in Partner's Fifth House/South Node in Eleventh House

To care for the needs of your soul, keep the fun, playfulness, and romance alive in your relationship. Your partner's natural way of living his or her life from the heart is a perfect fit for the path of your soul growth. Involvement with children and all aspects of creativity, either as patrons or performers, are also growth-oriented. The path of least resistance leads to taking each other for granted as casual friends, and missing the creative spark that comes from tickling each other's heart.

Your North Node in Partner's Sixth House/South Node in Twelfth House

Your partner's approach to tending to the affairs of everyday life is a good role model for your soul growth. The South Node placement shows you naturally understand how to help each other transcend the issues of everyday life to come to an understanding of the meaning and significance of it all. But in this life, you need to help each other show up to manage the affairs of everyday life. Growth comes through paying attention to what you can do to help each other's lives work more effectively in the here-and-now world of daily life. Participation in self-improvement programs together for either health or skill development would be ideal.

Your North Node in Partner's Seventh House/South Node in First House

Your partner's approach to relationships is right on track with what is growth-oriented for you. The path of soul growth is to bring honor and integrity into all of your agreements with each other. The process of coming to agreement and cooperative involvement is the path itself. The path of least resistance is to allow too much space for independent choices, thereby neglecting the process of negotiating, which is the high road of this path. Learning how to settle for nothing less than what is in your best interests, nor demanding more, in all cooperative endeavors is the path of growth.

Your North Node in Partner's Eighth House/South Node in Second House

Your path of soul growth in your partner's Eighth House of intimacy and shared resources leads to a deep relationship. Your partner's approach to intimacy is growth-oriented for you. The path of least resistance is to become so self-reliant that you miss the growth that comes from taking the emotional risks involved with intimacy and passion, or getting involved in each other's financial world. Growth comes through courting your partner's intimacy by creating a safe place within you for this to occur.

Your North Node in Partner's Ninth House/South Node in Third House

Your path of soul growth leads to cultivating the higher-mind aspects of the relationship with your partner. The path of least resistance is to become so chatty with each other that you miss the opportunity for growth available from cultivating philosophical interests in religion, spirituality, and politics. Travel together also expands the relationship beyond the familiar and is growth-oriented. To help each other expand beyond your existing beliefs is the path of growth, while encouraging each other to stay in the excessively familiar is the path of least resistance, with no growth. You know what your partner thinks; but do you know what he or she believes?

Your North Node in Partner's Tenth House/South Node in Fourth House

Your path of soul growth is to get involved in helping your partner rise to the heights of career potential. The path of least resistance is to draw exclusively on your familiarity and sense of history with each other, while missing opportunities for growth that come through helping each other reach for aspirations and make something of your lives. There is something about each other that reminds you both of your origins, roots, and personal history. This is a resource to draw upon, but it does not need to be nurtured. Nurturing each other's ambitions brings the growth your souls seek.

Your North Node in Partner's Eleventh House/South Node in Fifth House

The way your partner carries on friendship and social life is food for your soul. The path of soul growth is found in finding a greater purpose to your friendship beyond just having fun. The path of least resistance is spending so much time having fun and entertaining yourselves that you miss the opportunity for growth that would come through getting involved together in groups, causes, and larger social concerns.

Your North Node in Partner's Twelfth House/South Node in Sixth House

Your path of soul growth is to cultivate a spiritual relationship with your partner. Quality time alone together is the key, whether it involves nature, quiet activities, spiritual practices, or talking about each other's dreams. The path of least resistance is to get so caught up in putting out the fires of everyday existence that you fail to create retreat time together, and miss the opportunity for growth that could come from standing back from your lives and contemplating the meaning of what is going on.

27
Intra-Aspects and the Synastry Table

The aspects your planets make to another person's planets are the intra-aspects of the relationship. A synastry table is a grid with one person's planets listed at the top of the page horizontally, and the other person's planets listed vertically on the left of the page (chart 2). All of the major aspects between each other's planets are then listed in the grid. If you must calculate this by hand, it is tedious but doable. Thankfully, most astrology computer programs have this function, which makes this invaluable information readily accessible.

In this chapter you will find summary definitions of the aspects between the planets in your chart and those of your partner. To simplify, we will group the harmonious aspects together (sextile and trine) as well as the challenging aspects (square and opposition). The conjunction will be treated separately when the situation warrants, and grouped with the harmonious or challenging aspects when appropriate.

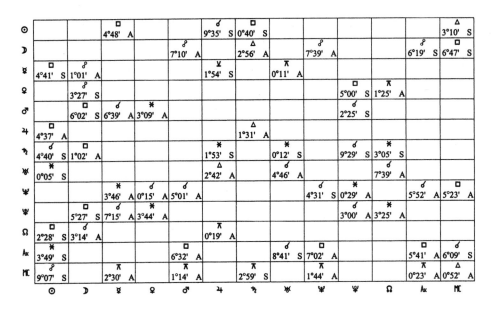

	☉	☽	☿	♀	♂	♃	♄	♅	♆	♇	☊	Asc	MC
☉			□ 4°48' A			☌ 9°35' S	□ 0°40' S						△ 3°10' S
☽					☍ 7°10' A		△ 2°56' A		☍ 7°39' A			☍ 6°19' S	□ 6°47' S
☿	□ 4°41' S	☍ 1°01' A				⚻ 1°54' S	⚻ 0°11' A						
♀		☍ 3°27' S								□ 5°00' S	⚻ 1°25' A		
♂		□ 6°02' S	☌ 6°39' A	✶ 3°09' A						☌ 2°25' S			
♃	□ 4°37' A						△ 1°31' A						
♄	☌ 4°40' S	□ 1°02' A				✶ 1°53' S	✶ 0°12' S			☌ 9°29' S	✶ 3°05' S		
♅	✶ 0°05' S					△ 2°42' A	☌ 4°46' A			☌ 7°39' A			
♆			✶ 3°46' A	☌ 0°15' A	☌ 5°01' A				☌ 4°31' S	✶ 0°29' A		☌ 5°52' A	□ 5°23' A
♇		□ 5°27' S	☌ 7°15' A	✶ 3°44' A					☌ 3°00' A	✶ 3°25' A			
☊	□ 2°28' S	☌ 3°14' A				⚻ 0°19' A							
Asc	✶ 3°49' S				□ 6°32' A			☌ 8°41' S	□ 7°02' A			□ 5°41' A	☌ 6°09' S
MC	☍ 9°07' S		⚻ 2°30' A		⚻ 1°14' A		⚻ 2°59' S		⚻ 1°44' A			⚻ 0°23' A	△ 0°52' S
	☉	☽	☿	♀	♂	♃	♄	♅	♆	♇	☊	Asc	MC

Chart 2

Synastry Table

Your Sun in Aspect to Partner's Moon

Conjunction

This is one of the more favorable and fertile aspects for a relationship. The Sun person projects energy in the same way the Moon person naturally responds—a perfect fit. I call this "cosmic glue," as there is something that just feels right about the overall relationship.

Harmonious

A natural flow exists in the relationship with your energies naturally supporting one another. The Moon person feels safe to drop defenses and be at ease around the Sun person's natural energy, allowing the Sun person to feel accepted and appreciated.

Challenging

The Moon person has a difficult time being emotionally at ease around the Sun person. This dynamic tension can manifest as rational arguments over emotional issues. The Sun person doesn't feel nurtured and the Moon person doesn't feel understood or at ease. The relationship functions best with some time apart in the daily schedule.

Your Sun in Aspect to Partner's Ascendant

Conjunction

This is another very favorable "cosmic glue" tie between charts. You both feel more confident, even physically stronger, when you are together. This can lead to a flowering of your personalities, as you both find new ways to express yourselves.

Harmonious

You enjoy and support each other's outlook on life, making it enjoyable to spend time together. Your personalities mix well.

Challenging (square)

Tension exists between the way you both approach situations, and there can be a conflict of will unless you allow for your differences.

Opposition

The opposition deserves special consideration, because this places the Sun on the partner's Seventh House cusp of relationships. While most oppositions are challenging, this one is very favorable for natural magnetic attraction between the two of you. You mirror and complement each other's perspective.

Your Sun in Aspect to Partner's Mercury

Harmonious (including conjunction)

Communication and a natural understanding of each other are favored. You "get" each other and readily resolve the natural conflicts that arise in relationships. You stimulate each other's mental activity and readily learn from each other.

Challenging

Communication difficulties arise because of the angular nature of your perspective on issues. You see things differently and must allow for this if the relationship is to flourish. Otherwise, petty arguments could arise over how things are said to each other.

Your Sun in Aspect to Partner's Venus

Harmonious (particularly the conjunction)

This is one of the sweet ties in relationship astrology, leading to natural affection and simply enjoying being in each other's company. If it's not a romantic relationship, the arts and cultural opportunities are a few of a multitude of ways to share and enjoy life with each other. The natural magnetic flow of attraction that exists between the two of you makes it easier to overlook each other's shortcomings.

Challenging

Your tastes and values can clash, and yet this is not entirely bad. It creates a strong sexual attraction, though not the comfortable type; this type of fascination comes from that which is different. The strong sexual attraction is favorable for getting the relationship going, but difficulties can arise over differences in basic life values, making it difficult to live with each other on a day-to-day basis.

Your Sun in Aspect to Partner's Mars

Harmonious

You are able to work and play well together, because the way you do things doesn't get in each other's way. You rarely have a conflict of wills and readily resolve issues when they arise. You naturally empower each other's courage and your passions flow well together.

Challenging (including conjunction)

This tie is extremely intense and often confrontational. The conjunction is not particularly bad, but often too hot to handle. It is passionate, without a doubt, and very favorable in some arenas, but arguments and battles of will can be passionate as well. If you can't take the heat, get out of the kitchen, with this one. You can inflame each other, and without restraint or healthy outlets, things could turn bad.

Your Sun in Aspect to Partner's Jupiter

Harmonious (including conjunction)

You encourage a positive outlook on life together and there is no end to the number of growth-oriented activities that you could enjoy together. You both feel confident that it is safe to trust each other. Shared experiences with travel, education, and philosophical pursuits are favored.

Challenging

You can encourage excessiveness in each other, one way or another. The Jupiter person may try to encourage the Sun person to grow and expand in ways that are not appropriate. This is motivational for individuals who do not want to settle for complacency and, instead, reach for more of what life has to offer, but watch out for grasping.

Your Sun in Aspect to Partner's Saturn

Conjunction

This tie can go one of two ways. First, the restraining and restricting nature of the Saturn person can have a dampening influence on the Sun person, who can feel the Saturn person to be a heavy responsibility. However, this same aspect is often found in profound, long-term relationships where both feel a deep commitment and sense of loyalty to each other. If the Saturn person is the repressive type, the Sun person will feel it immediately. This is most favorable in mentor situations where it is appropriate for the Saturn person to hold the authority in the relationship.

Harmonious

You have patience with each other and can work well together either professionally or when sharing life's responsibilities. You can even be patient with each other's "bad" days. You learn from your experiences together and typically don't make the same mistakes twice with each other.

Challenging

The Sun person feels the hammer of the Saturn's person disapproval always close at hand. The Saturn person gets irritated with the Sun person's lack of responsibility. Projections abound between the two of you, and the wise person sees the very qualities you dislike in each other as projections of unclaimed parts of your own character. It takes character strength to deal successfully with this one; otherwise the Sun person can feel disapproved of and the Saturn person feels unappreciated.

Your Sun in Aspect to Partner's Uranus

Conjunction

There is something electric, exciting, and liberating about your relationship with each other. You encourage each other to cast off cultural expectations and pursue your authentic natures. Although exciting, Uranus is a wild card and the unsettledness and uncertainty that comes with Uranus is part of the territory.

Harmonious

You encourage and support each other's uniqueness and individuality and put very few restraints and expectations on each other. This allows your relationship to continue to grow and evolve.

Challenging

This tie creates a strong fascination, but is considered unstable. Your wills can clash over the slightest of issues, as you both absolutely resist either of your attempts to take charge in the relationship. The relationship requires a great deal of freedom to make room for this aspect.

Your Sun in Aspect to Partner's Neptune

Conjunction

There is something mystical and spiritual about your tie, although it can be equally mystifying as mystical. It is best for couples involved with spiritual or artistic activities together, where the imagination does some good. There can be a telepathic, psychic rapport if you allow it. You must watch out for soap-bubble dreams and all types of illusions with imaginative Neptune activated in the relationship.

Harmonious

There is a natural intuitive flow between the two of you that is quite comfortable. You can be drawn to understand the subtle realms together through meditation and spiritual practices. You empower each other's faith in listening to the "still, small voice within."

Challenging

It is not likely that you see each other clearly. Neptune is the blind spot, and when challenging the Sun, you can lead each other into illusions. The Neptune person sees qualities that may, or may not, be in the Sun person. The Sun person can look at the Neptune person as being totally ungrounded in reality.

Your Sun in Aspect to Partner's Pluto

Conjunction

This is an extremely powerful aspect that has to be handled wisely. The Pluto person's will has a subconscious impact on the Sun person. The relationship can facilitate major transformation; rarely would it be casual. There can seem to be something fated or karmic about this tie, unleashing a tremendous amount of power and passion between the two of you. If this is healthy, bravo, this can be an extremely profound relationship. If either person feels threatened in any way by the other, not much good can come from the tie.

Harmonious

The relationship feels safe, as feelings of threat drop away when you are together. You are there for each other when destiny calls to lend strength. You help each other stay on track with your higher purpose in life.

Challenging

Power struggles are likely to erupt unless both of you stay vigilant for any attempts by the other to control the relationship in any way. The Sun person can feel that the Pluto person is always pulling strings trying to get something. The Pluto person can feel as if the Sun person is always challenging his or her authority.

Your Sun in Aspect to Partner's Nodes

Conjunction to North Node (opposite South Node)

The Sun person naturally supports a path for the North Node person that is growth-oriented and food for the soul. It doesn't mean you are always comfortable with each other; in fact, sometimes it can feel like a stretch into the unfamiliar, but it is a healthy growth-oriented stretch that you encourage in each other.

Conjunction to South Node (opposite North Node)

There can be something deeply familiar about each other when you first meet, as if you are picking up where you left off. Although this familiarity leads to the likelihood of some type of relationship, if you don't encourage new growth in each other, the relationship can wither from its own redundancy.

Harmonious to Both Nodes

You naturally support each other's path toward soul growth. This happens without effort. You are able to help each other glean valuable lessons from your personal histories, freeing you from having to repeat the past.

Challenging (square)

The relationship goes through periods where growth seems to be stalled and you pull each other into past patterns. Are you going to support each other's growth, or hold each other to the past?

Your Moon in Aspect to Partner's Ascendant

Conjunction

You are strongly impacted by each other's moods and emotional cycles. This gives you natural empathy for each other, but makes it difficult for either of you to remain objective when emotions arise.

Harmonious

You feel at ease and comfortable in each other's presence. This relaxed flow between the two of you allows you to spend considerable time with each other.

Challenging

Misunderstandings often arise when the emotional needs of the Moon person are expressed in a way that irritates the Ascendant person. Your relationship benefits from spending a little time apart in the daily schedule to avoid getting on each other's nerves.

Your Moon in Aspect to Partner's Mercury

Conjunction

You two can communicate about the most personal of issues, because the Mercury person's communication style allows the Moon person to feel totally comfortable sharing feelings. The Moon person helps the Mercury person get in touch with the emotional considerations of important issues, and the Mercury person helps the Moon person see the objective perspective to emotional issues.

Harmonious

Communication over personal issues is favored. You can always depend on each other for understanding when needed, and this brings clarity into your lives.

Challenging

Communication over emotional issues is difficult. The Moon person reads meaning into the words of the Mercury person that wasn't intended. The Mercury person has difficulty understanding the emotional needs of the Moon person. Rational arguments over emotional issues are likely. Words often don't help in clearing up misunderstandings; try silence . . . look into each other's eyes, silently communicate your intent to get through the issue, hold each other . . . it works.

Your Moon in Aspect to Partner's Venus

Conjunction

This aspect could be characterized as "sweet." It is easy to trust one another and romance is likely. Simply spending time together is emotionally rewarding and even delightful. The personal side of life is favored.

Harmonious

You can feel very natural and comfortable in each other's presence, making time spent together enjoyable. You support and even take delight in each other's emotional responses to life. You can become interested in the arts and socializing together.

Challenging

Emotional issues are quite tricky to resolve. When one of you expresses emotional needs, the other person's feelings get hurt. Or you get your feelings hurt when the other person is simply having a bad day. It is hard not to take the other person's emotional issues personally, but that is exactly what can improve your relationship.

Your Moon in Aspect to Partner's Mars

Conjunction

This is a hot, passionate, and volatile combination. The Moon person can feel picked on and badgered by the Mars person. The Mars person can have angry eruptions over the emotional responses of the Moon person. If you can handle the heat, passion and intensity are assured.

Harmonious

The Moon person feels safe and protected by the Mars person's strength. The Mars person feels emotionally supported in choices of action. You rarely trigger each other's defenses.

Challenging

This aspect often leads to a stormy emotional tie. The Moon person is always on edge and feels threatened by the Mars person's energy. The emotional responses of the Moon person irritate the Mars person. Without restraint, this can be a wounding combination.

Your Moon in Aspect to Partner's Jupiter

Harmonious (including conjunction)

The Jupiter person has a knack for uplifting the mood of the Moon person. The Moon person, of course, enjoys this, so a positive, trusting relationship develops. The Moon person emotionally supports the growth needs and the philosophical and religious interests of the Jupiter person.

Challenging

You tend to encourage each other's indulgent behavior. There can be excessive emotional reactions over small issues that get blown way out of proportion.

Your Moon in Aspect to Partner's Saturn

Conjunction

The Moon person feels the pressure of the Saturn person's expectations and judgments, and thus is extremely sensitive to his or her approval and disapproval. If handled wisely, this creates a strong sense of responsibility that binds the two of you together. If not handled wisely, the Moon person feels unsafe in emotional expression, and close interaction can be blocked.

Harmonious

You work well together on both the personal and professional fronts. The Saturn person gives steadiness and patience to the relationship. The Moon person adds emotional support to the Saturn person's efforts in the world of responsibility.

Challenging

This tie is usually considered unfavorable for emotional relationships, unless the Saturn person is mindful of the excessive sensitivity the Moon person has to any disapproval.

The Moon person's emotional needs are judged as weak by the Saturn person and tend to go unmet.

Your Moon in Aspect to Partner's Uranus

Conjunction

This tie could be described as exciting and electric, but not comfortable. The Uranus person liberates the Moon person from the confines of past behavior patterns, but it is hard for the Moon person to ever feel fully comfortable and secure around the unpredictable Uranus person.

Harmonious

This is an aspect that encourages evolutionary growth on both your parts. The Moon person feels encouraged and supported for breaking out of old emotional patterns, and the Uranus person feels emotionally supported for pursuing an authentic path of individuality.

Challenging

The Moon person tends to feel threatened by the Uranus person's independence and need for freedom, while the Uranus person feels encumbered by the emotional needs of the Moon person.

Your Moon in Aspect to Partner's Neptune

Conjunction

A highly intuitive, nearly psychic tie exists between the two of you. Romantic, spiritual, and imaginative are the high-road qualities of this connection. You will have to take care not to project fantasies onto each other and watch out for a tendency to avoid unpleasant issues.

Harmonious

An empathic rapport between the two of you is likely. The Neptune person helps the Moon person rise above petty issues, and Moon person helps the Neptune person stay in touch with personal feelings.

Challenging

It is not likely that you see each other clearly. You can imagine qualities in each other that don't exist, or pull each other into escapist behavior, or feed each other's fears. Absolute honesty, including avoiding "dishonesty by omission," is required for a healthy relationship.

Your Moon in Aspect to Partner's Pluto

Harmonious

You give each other the emotional strength to make important transformations in life. The Moon person feels safe and unthreatened by the Pluto person's use of power. The Pluto person feels comforted by the Moon person's support.

Challenging (including conjunction)

The Moon person can feel threatened, unsafe, and powerless to withstand the Pluto's person's will. A healthy relationship can develop only if the Pluto person can remain conscious of the potential misuse of this power of intimidation. Otherwise, the potential for unhealthy psychological patterns to develop between the two of you is strong.

Your Moon in Aspect to Partner's Nodes

Conjunction to North Node (opposite South Node)

The Moon person's natural emotional responses to life are nurturing for the path of soul growth for the North Node person. This tie is not particularly comfortable because it is a growth-oriented aspect, rather than one of familiarity.

Conjunction to South Node (opposite North Node)

This points to the likelihood of strong family karma from past lives impacting your relationship. Something akin to *déjà vu* starts the relationship off on a strong note, but it is difficult to pull out of the past and keep growing in your relationship. The Moon person can feel drained by the needs of the South Node person unless you both stay vigilant about keeping to a path of growth and overcoming past behavior patterns.

Harmonious to Both Nodes

You both naturally support each other's soul growth, but this aspect is different from the conjunction in that you feel familiar and comfortable with each other.

Challenging (square)

Your relationship could be characterized as "one step forward, two steps back," as you periodically pull each other into past emotional patterns, and can feel threatened by each other's growth.

Your Ascendant in Aspect to Partner's Ascendant

Conjunction

Your approaches to life are perfectly aligned with each other. This similar attitude is echoed through the other houses in your charts as well, enhancing your overall compatibility.

Harmonious

Your approaches to life are in harmony with each other, making it enjoyable and easy to spend time together. You both feel supported in your outlook on life.

Challenging

Your attitudes about approaching most everything conflict with each other. To have a healthy relationship, you both are forced to stretch your acceptance of these differences to offset the tendency to get irritated with each other.

Your Ascendant in Aspect to Partner's Mercury

Conjunction

This aspect is very beneficial for communication. The Ascendant person feels free to express himself or herself to the Mercury person like with no other. This greatly enhances the ability to communicate through difficulties.

Harmonious

You have a natural understanding of each other and feel free to express yourselves to each other, knowing you will be understood.

Challenging

Misunderstandings are not uncommon with this aspect, as you both tend to misinterpret each other's attempts at communication. Avoid this potential for misunderstanding by double-checking important communications with each other.

Your Ascendant in Aspect to Partner's Venus

Harmonious (including conjunction)

This is a highly magnetic and sweet combination. The Venus person is very attracted to the looks and style of the Ascendant person. It is easy to love one another, and interests in the arts, entertainment, and culture are favored.

Challenging

Your values and sensitivities to beauty clash with one another. The Ascendant person's natural style of presentation is a turn-off for the Venus person. The Venus person can seem uptight to the Ascendant person.

Your Ascendant in Aspect to Partner's Mars

Conjunction

This is a hot, intense, and potentially sexual combination. The Mars person is motivational, giving backbone and courage to the Ascendant person. The Ascendant person admires the strength and courage of the Mars person. The Mars person will have to be careful not to be overly motivational/pushy. Shared physical activities are favored.

Harmonious

Your energies flow well together, making it easy to work or play together. You rarely trigger each other's defenses, allowing you feel safe with each other. Knowing you can count on each other's support in any conflict gives you courage.

Challenging

Conflicts erupt when the Ascendant person feels picked on or badgered by the Mars person. Conversely, the Mars person becomes irritated by the Ascendant person's approach to situations.

Your Ascendant in Aspect to Partner's Jupiter

Conjunction

This is a very uplifting combination. The Jupiter person helps the Ascendant person maintain a positive perspective on life, and feels appreciated by the Ascendant person. Travel and educational pursuits together are favored.

Harmonious

This aspect is favorable for most relationships as the two of you share common philosophical, political, and religious beliefs, as well as cultural interests. It simply feels uplifting to be in each other's company.

Challenging

Many disagreements can erupt because your basic beliefs about so many life issues are at odds with each other. These arguments aren't so hot as to be threatening, with Jupiter involved, but the Ascendant person can experience the Jupiter person's beliefs about education, religion, and politics to be way off base.

Your Ascendant in Aspect to Partner's Saturn

Conjunction

The Saturn person is a natural authority for the Ascendant person; thus, this is a favorable tie for parent-child, employer-employee, and teacher-student relationships, when the Saturn person is the authority. There is a strong commitment and sense of loyalty that comes with this tie, but the Ascendant person can feel oppressed by the Saturn person unless this authority is handled wisely and the hammer of disapproval is used sparingly.

Harmonious

This is a stabilizing aspect for all relationships. The Saturn person is patient with the Ascendant person and can be a source of guidance without being heavy-handed. The Ascendant person helps the Saturn person stay focused on manifesting ambitions and goals. This combination is excellent for being able to work through the difficult times together on any type of commitment.

Challenging

The Ascendant person feels disempowered by the Saturn person's disapproval. You can both feel disrespected for what you stand for. The relationship feels strained unless you overcome your judgments of each other.

Your Ascendant in Aspect to Partner's Uranus

Conjunction

This aspect is liberating and electric, though somewhat unpredictable, in its impact. The Uranus person encourages the Ascendant person to break free from convention and become more individualistic in personal style. The Ascendant person encourages the Uranus person to act on original ideas.

Harmonious

You encourage and support each other's uniqueness and individuality by giving each other permission to be just who you are without pretension. You support each other's path of awakening and evolution by encouraging each other to stay in an attitude of discovery.

Challenging

This destabilizing aspect will keep your relationship from becoming stagnant, if nothing else. The Ascendant person feels uncomfortable with, and even threatened by, the way the Uranus person expresses individuality and independence. The Uranus person constantly hammers at the conventionality of the Ascendant person.

Your Ascendant in Aspect to Partner's Neptune

Conjunction

A highly intuitive, mystical, and psychic connection exists between the two of you. Relationships that include artistic and spiritual pursuits are highly favored. If neither person is skilled in a healthy use of the imagination, this aspect can create illusions about the relationship that are not grounded in reality. Make sure you consider the whole picture, best- and worst-case scenarios, before acting on your inspirations together to avoid the dangers of Neptune's blind spot.

Harmonious

This is a favorable aspect that allows the Neptune person to help the Ascendant person rise above petty issues, and the Ascendant person to help the Neptune person follow spiritual and creative vision. Involvements in the arts and spiritual activity together are highly favored.

Challenging

A lack of clarity between the two of you can cloud the relationship. You likely misinterpret each other, and difficulties arise over illusions that one or both of you have about each other and the relationship. Honesty is essential, even if conflict erupts; better to deal with the issues and stay clear than to pretend there aren't any issues and remain in illusion.

Your Ascendant in Aspect to Partner's Pluto

Conjunction

This is a powerful and transformative combination that, if used wisely, can help you both shed what you are not, and become what you are meant to be. The Pluto person's will has a tremendous impact and influence on the Ascendant person's outlook on life. The low road would lead to manipulative behavior by the Pluto person with this influence.

Harmonious

You support the deepest type of spiritual transformation in each other and can be a source of hidden strength for each other.

Challenging

The Ascendant person can feel intimidated by the Pluto person because of something that neither of you is conscious of. This makes it difficult to have a relationship until trust is established. You see each other's idiosyncrasies and subconscious behavior patterns. It takes great sensitivity of delivery to discuss such issues without arousing your partner's defenses.

Your Ascendant in Aspect to Partner's Nodes

Conjunction to North Node (opposite South Node)

This combination can lead to soul growth for both of you, although is doesn't always make for a comfortable relationship because of the lack of familiarity with each other's orientation to life. The Ascendant person's natural way of approaching life merges with the path of soul growth for the North Node person, creating a fertile combination for continued spiritual growth for both of you.

Conjunction to South Node (opposite North Node)

There is something hauntingly familiar about each other, and it is easy to get to know one another because of this. The path of least resistance is to get caught up in the presentation and looks of the relationship, while the path of growth is to cultivate substance.

Harmonious to Both Nodes

This allows for an easy, growth-oriented approach to life together. Your natural pursuits and interests support each other's soul growth.

Challenging (square)

It is sometimes difficult to stay on a growth-oriented path together because personality conflicts periodically pull each of you down into past behavior patterns.

Your Mercury in Aspect to Partner's Venus

Harmonious (including conjunction)

This creates a stimulating spark in your exchanges as you both enjoy each other's personality. The Mercury person communicates in a way that the Venus person enjoys, and thus friendship and romance are favored. Creative outlets are also favored, although any relationship and any activity would benefit from this delightful combination.

Challenging

The Mercury person communicates in a way that offends the sensibilities of the Venus person. The Mercury person feels the Venus person is pretentious. The Venus person gets hurt feelings over the way the Mercury person communicates. You would be advised to educate each other as to these sensitivities to avoid them in the future.

Your Mercury in Aspect to Partner's Mars

Conjunction

This aspect leads to passionate, intense communication between the two of you that can also be volatile if not directed wisely. The Mars person motivates the Mercury person to act on ideas, and the Mercury person brings ideas and information to the Mars person's activities. All of this is favorable when it leads to action. The trigger for volatility is that the Mars person can seem intimidating, overbearing, and even hostile to the Mercury person unless the Mars person is able to exercise restraint when the Mercury person is giving signals of being overwhelmed.

Harmonious

This tie is favorable for motivating you both to act on ideas. You rarely trigger each other's defenses in communications, and can even work through difficult moments together without feeling threatened by each other.

Challenging

This aspect sets up arguments, because you tend to constantly trigger each other's defenses. The way the Mercury person thinks and makes decisions can irritate the Mars person, while the Mercury person constantly feels badgered and provoked by the will of the Mars person. Learning how to avoid reacting to each other so quickly is a key. When you feel hostility from each other, quiet it in yourself before you react, and you can avoid the knee-jerk arguments that this aspect is known for.

Your Mercury in Aspect to Partner's Jupiter

Harmonious (including conjunction)

This aspect is very favorable for communication and mutual interests in continued learning. The philosophical outlook on life of the Jupiter person is expansive and uplifting to the Mercury person. The Mercury person engages the philosophical beliefs of the Jupiter person and helps plan movement toward goals.

Challenging

Your learning styles are significantly different enough that it makes it difficult to carry out intellectual projects together without getting exasperated with each other. The Jupiter person is interested in growth that doesn't interest the Mercury person. The Mercury person can seem narrow-minded and picky to the Jupiter person. Give space for your different learning styles and interests to avoid conflict.

Your Mercury in Aspect to Partner's Saturn

Conjunction

This aspect is favorable for making important business decisions together, or doing serious research on some important interest. It is not so favorable for just having fun together, with the Saturn person's serious ways being brought into communications. This combination works best when the Saturn person is a natural authority for the Mercury person, but not so favorable the other way around.

Harmonious

You are able to handle responsibilities well together. You not only make plans well, you are able to follow through on them with patience and commitment. When difficulties in your relationship do arise, this combination facilitates an ability to work through the issues patiently.

Challenging

This aspect creates a challenge in maintaining easy, flowing communication with each other, because the Mercury person feels intimidated by the judgments of the Saturn person. This fear of disapproval restricts the natural flow of conversation. There is a tendency to bring out each other's pessimistic and negative attitudes. This can be compensated for, but there would have to be a rule: *No criticizing each other*. Otherwise, this combination is a tough one.

Your Mercury in Aspect to Partner's Uranus

Conjunction

This is a very exciting connection for communication and learning together. The Uranus person's energy liberates the Mercury person's way of thinking, though it does make it difficult to stay on the topic at hand. While in conversations with each other, ideas just come flying in about all types of issues, not just what you are currently discussing. Some of the ideas that you come up with together are likely to be out of synch with your culture, so it's best to think things through before you act on some of your radical ideas.

Harmonious

You two are excellent at looking at issues from a fresh perspective and coming up with innovative ideas for dealing with situations. Your communications stay lively as you encourage a "discovery" attitude in each other. The ideas that you come up with together most often have relevance and application in your lives.

Challenging

A tension exists in your communications with each other. The Uranus person wants the Mercury person to change the way she or he thinks about something in a way that is inconceivable to the Mercury person. The Mercury person can feel the Uranus person to be a disruptive, unruly influence, and the Uranus person can view the Mercury person as narrow-minded and stuck in conventional thinking.

Your Mercury in Aspect to Partner's Neptune

Conjunction

This leads to a mystical, nearly psychic connection between the two of you. Mutual interests in mysticism, spirituality, and artistic pursuits are favored. Worldly issues and practical concerns are not so favored. In these issues, it is best to compensate for this imaginative combination by making sure that you are not seeing potential that doesn't really exist.

Harmonious

You have a highly intuitive rapport with each other. This supports your communication, allowing you get the subtle nuances. You help each other rise above petty issues and can encourage each other's interests in spirituality and the arts.

Challenging

Your communication with each other can become clouded by confusion, mostly over what was not said. Fact and fantasy blur. It may not be clear what was said and not said, what is true or not true; these types of issues cause the confusion. Absolute honesty is required to avoid these pitfalls.

Your Mercury in Aspect to Partner's Pluto

Conjunction

At best, this aspect leads to profound depth in all mental pursuits together. At worst, the Mercury person feels manipulated and even intimidated by the Pluto person's power. This combination is excellent for research and investigation into almost anything, particularly the occult and metaphysical.

Harmonious

This tie is favorable for pursuing mental activities together, and you feel safe with each other in taking conversations to a deep, intimate level. You likely feel comfortable revealing personal secrets to each other.

Challenging

Difficulties in communications with each other arise because of the Mercury person's tendency to feel threatened by the Pluto person's will. It is important not to allow manipulations of any sort to enter into your communications with each other; no good can come from it. If either of you feels manipulated by the other, name it for what it is, and refuse to take part in it.

Your Mercury in Aspect to Partner's Nodes

Conjunction to South Node (opposite North Node)

Getting to know each other will be like picking up where you left off. You carry the past-life karma of siblings or students on a path together, which is considered favorable in the range of past-life karma. Although this tie is favorable for starting a relationship, you will need to encourage each other to continue to learn and grow to avoid the tendency to hold each other back in the past.

Harmonious (including conjunction to North Node)

Your conversations and mental pursuits together naturally lead to each other's soul growth. You can draw on each other for support and understanding in spiritual issues.

Challenging (square)

This push-pull combination impacts the communication patterns in the relationship. You periodically support each other's growth, and periodically pull each other back to things that were said in the past. Extra effort is required to learn from your challenges and move on; otherwise, haunting issues from the past can pull the relationship down.

Your Venus in Aspect to Partner's Mars

Conjunction

Strong sexual attraction is always present with this "cosmic glue" combination. Even when you're upset with each other emotionally or mentally, your bodies would just as soon be hugging. The only danger of this tie is taking this magnetism for granted and failing to cultivate the ongoing courtship required to sustain the initial spark.

Harmonious

There is very favorable magnetic flow between the two of you that could best be described as delightful. This creates an energetic spark that is well received by both of you. You are skilled at keeping this spark of magnetism alive long into your relationship.

Challenging

There is a magnetic spark between you, without a doubt, but it is sometimes rough and has an edge. This is good for passion, but is volatile because so many of your values about male/female roles in a relationship clash.

Your Venus in Aspect to Partner's Jupiter

Conjunction

Fertile, abundant, and indulgent are all words that could describe this combination. Your love life is upbeat and positive together, and it's easy to enjoy each other's company. It would be easy to fall in love. The only danger with this extremely positive combination is the tendency toward excessive indulgences and spending sprees together.

Harmonious

The friendship between the two of you flows naturally and you encourage movement toward refinement in each other's life. The arts, culture, philosophy, and socializing together are all favored.

Challenging

It is not always easy to find ways to socialize together. What one of you considers a growth-oriented activity, the other might not value at all. When you do get together, there is the risk of encouraging each other's excessive behavior.

Your Venus in Aspect to Partner's Saturn

Conjunction

The best of this aspect is a serious, commitment-based relationship with a strong sense of responsibility for each other. The worst of it is if the Venus person feels disapproval from the Saturn person, making the flow of love difficult. When at odds with each other, the Venus person can feel the Saturn person to be an oppressive responsibility more than a joyful companion, and the Saturn person can view the Venus person as undisciplined and indulgent, and needing to learn restraint.

Harmonious

This aspect adds stability to your relationship because you have the patience and commitment it takes to work through the rough spots. You complement each other's lives, as the Venus person brings out the personal side of the Saturn person, and the Saturn person helps the Venus person keep it together in the world.

Challenging

This aspect dampens the natural attraction and magnetism of the relationship. It is hard to avoid judging one another. The Venus person looks at the Saturn person as no fun, too harsh, and demanding, while the Saturn person judges the Venus person's values as superficial, indulgent, and undisciplined.

Your Venus in Aspect to Partner's Uranus

Conjunction

This creates an electric magnetism between the two of you, but it is highly unstable. The Uranus person liberates the Venus person from conventional attitudes, and the Venus person is excited by the uniqueness of the Uranus person. The unpredictable nature of the Uranus person keeps a tone of uncertainty in the relationship.

Harmonious

Your relationship will never be in danger of stagnating because you constantly find innovative ways to explore life together. You are attracted to each other's uniqueness and allow each other considerable freedom in the relationship.

Challenging

The Uranus person feels constrained by the Venus person's values and attitudes about relationships. The Venus person's security is threatened by the Uranus person's need for freedom. There can be sexual magnetism that comes from the fascination of something different, but your tastes being so different would be a test.

Your Venus in Aspect to Partner's Neptune

Conjunction

Here, two levels of love are linked together. Venus is personal, romantic love. Neptune is spiritual love. At the highest level, there is the opportunity for sacred sexuality in your union. You will have to watch out for illusions, however, as this can lead to falling in love with qualities that you only imagine are there in the other person.

Harmonious

This aspect brings a refined energy into your relationship, and you become sensitive to the subtle realms of your energy with each other. A peaceful feeling flows between the two of you, and you can enjoy the arts, music, and spiritual activities together.

Challenging

There can be a mystical attraction between the two of you, but there is the danger of illusions and deception with this combination. Fantasy can be delightful in love when it is a seasoning, but when it is the main course, disillusionment is the ultimate result when the fantasy can't be sustained in reality.

Your Venus in Aspect to Partner's Pluto

Conjunction

A compelling, nearly hypnotic attraction can exist between the two of you. With highly developed souls, this can lead to deep, transformative passion. With lower types, the compelling energy can lead to obsessions or manipulative love.

Harmonious

The current of sexual magnetism between the two of you runs deep. You both heal effectively from wounding times together, giving your relationship strong regenerative abilities. Money and financial dealings with each other are also favored.

Challenging

Karmic patterns of manipulating each other in love, either through guilt or intimidation, must be dealt with in your relationship. Strong passion can exist between the two of you, but intimacy will elude you until you are both able to let go of control and surrender to the relationship.

Your Venus in Aspect to Partner's Nodes

Conjunction to South Node (opposite North Node)

The past-life karma you bring into this life is that of the Venus person having been a female lover for the South Node person in a previous life. It is easy to love one another, but soul memories stir feelings that don't make sense in this life. Will you promote soul growth for each other in this life, or will you cling to memories and yearnings for how things were?

Harmonious (including conjunction to North Node)

Your values and tastes are in harmony with one another, and you are naturally attracted to activities that lead to mutual soul growth.

Challenging (square)

Your tastes, both in terms of pleasure and soul-growth activities, are not in synch with each other. Since neither of you values the other person's taste in clothes, style, art, beauty, and social activities, this aspect has a diminishing effect on the magnetism between you.

Your Mars in Aspect to Partner's Jupiter

Conjunction

Your relationship is fueled with tremendous drive, passion for life, and competitive energy. The Jupiter person expands the awareness of the field of opportunities for the Mars person. The Mars person gives courage to the Jupiter person for acting on goals and ideals. Your relationship requires action, or the heated-up and expanded energy can become volatile.

Harmonious

You bring out a confident and positive attitude in each other, allowing you to work and play well together. You also travel well together and encourage each other to take part in the opportunities life has to offer.

Challenging

Although not a hostile aspect, you can provoke a competitive reaction in each other. You tend to exacerbate each other's issues with impatience and rash behavior. Arguments could flare up over differences in political and religious views. It would be helpful to weave some healthy, playful competition into your relationship to vent this dynamic energy.

Your Mars in Aspect to Partner's Saturn

Conjunction

The Saturn person restricts and restrains the energy expression of the Mars person. This is typically frustrating for the Mars person who feels blocked at every turn by the Saturn person. This is best when the Saturn person is a natural authority figure for the Mars person, such as coach, parent, boss, or mentor, but even in these roles, trouble will erupt if there isn't mutual respect.

Harmonious

This aspect is excellent for working on difficult projects together, or anything that requires patience and determination. This gives strength and backbone to the relationship, allowing you to get through the difficult times without falling apart.

Challenging

This is one of the red flags to watch out for in synastry. The potential for angry flare-ups is strong. The Mars person feels pressured and disapproved of by the Saturn person, fueling anger and resentment. The Saturn person feels the Mars person is purposefully trying to be a source of aggravation and irritation. To avoid the defensive reactions that are sure to be there otherwise, it is essential to avoid correcting each other's behavior.

Your Mars in Aspect to Partner's Uranus

Conjunction

The Uranus person's liberating influence on the Mars person makes all options available. Excitement comes from this. So will unexpected flare-ups of wild, uncontrollable energy. There can be excitement in a sexual relationship as you encourage each other's experimentation. If you can't handle the intensity, this unrestrained energy can manifest as explosive fights between the two of you that scare you both with the fierceness that comes over you. If handled well, you will give each other courage to act on your most innovative ideas.

Harmonious

You encourage each other's independence and have marvelous improvisational skills together. In romance, you take delight in each other's exploratory and innovative sexual style.

Challenging

This is another red flag aspect that requires skill to avoid the danger. Wild, unexpected conflicts can rise up between the two of you like spring thunderstorms, so you have to be careful not to set each other off. You can encourage reckless behavior in each other unless you learn to handle these surges of intense energy that flare up between the two of you.

Your Mars in Aspect to Partner's Neptune

Conjunction

The best of this aspect would lead to inspired activity together. Music, dance, tai chi, and creative spiritual outlets of all sorts are the fruits of aligning with the high road of this combination. However, Neptune is also known as the blind spot, and it is important to know the risk of making poor choices of action together. This aspect can bring a mystical quality to your passion, and at minimum, imagination is brought into love play. Trust this combination with creativity and the like where the imagination is not troublesome, but be cautious of this same imagination in worldly affairs involving money and finance where there can be a stiff price to pay for poor judgment.

Harmonious

This combination is excellent for romance as it brings the best of imagination into your passion. You can inspire each other creatively in all types of ways, and the danger of seeing potential that doesn't exist is minimized.

Challenging

This is a difficult aspect because of its insidious qualities. The source of problems and conflicts between the two of you is never obvious. As lovers, you can bring out a fascination for eroticism in each other, but you are not each other's best counsel in making important decisions, as this aspect brings out the worst of the blind spot phenomenon of Neptune aspects. Deception on one or both of your parts is also a possible negative manifestation of this energy.

Your Mars in Aspect to Partner's Pluto

Conjunction

This is an extremely powerful aspect, for good or ill. The high road leads to an invincible will when this power is focused in honorable directions together. Passion can top the charts in a healthy sexual relationship. The saying "Power corrupts" describes the low road manifestations of this combination. In worst-case scenarios, violence could erupt. Encouraging each other's attitude of "Might makes right" could lead to all types of misuses of this energy. If you can't direct the energy in healthy directions, all types of strange obsessions with each other could manifest.

Harmonious

You draw hidden strength from each other and thus are great allies for one another. You inspire each other to the right use of will and power in ways that benefit everyone. Whether engaging in shared physical activities or exploring the deep mysteries of psychology and the occult together, you feel safe with each other.

Challenging

You are being tested with the right use of power in this relationship, and power conflicts erupt with the slightest provocation on either of your parts. Taking martial arts training together would be a good metaphor of your test. With this training you would learn that your power comes from staying in your center, and not getting pulled into anger. This is no small trick in your relationship because of the hair-trigger reactions you both have to conflict issues when either of you tries to change the other in any way. You can bring out each other's shadow issues, and need to be willing to question your motives in any plans you come up with together.

Your Mars in Aspect to Partner's Nodes

Harmonious (including conjunction to North Node)

You keep each other current with the times and on track with your soul growth. You give each other courage to move forward, away from the path of least resistance and toward growth.

Challenging (square)

The Mars person's choices of activities are often off track for the path of soul growth for the Nodal person. You would be advised to allow space in your relationship for your separate interests.

Conjunction to South Node (opposite North Node)

Your relationship brings the past-life karma of the Mars person having been a strong male in the South Node person's past life. Lover? Combative adversary? Source of courage? You will know if the connection is favorable or not. If there is underlying anger that periodically worms its way into your current relationship, it might very well be residual past-life karma between the two of you. It would take deep forgiveness on both of your parts for all past wounds, known and unknown, complete amnesty, to clear the slate and have an honest go of it in this life.

Your Jupiter in Aspect to Partner's Saturn

Conjunction

The best of this aspect leads to controlled growth in the relationship. The Saturn person provides the appropriate structure and restraint for the Jupiter person to be successful in following through on plans. The Jupiter person gives the Saturn person confidence to fulfill responsibilities. The low road leads to the Saturn person squelching the goals and optimism of the Jupiter person.

Harmonious

You work well together on career and professional matters, as well as all issues of handling responsibility together. You are especially effective at planning together and follow a step-by-step approach to reaching your shared goals.

Challenging

Your sense of timing is not likely to be in synch with each other; when one of you wants to expand, the other wants to hold back. You may have many conflicting views about politics, religion, business ethics, and the like, making it difficult to support each other's plans.

Your Jupiter in Aspect to Partner's Uranus

Conjunction

This aspect creates excitement between the two of you about the soon-to-be-discovered future. You both have the potential to be a liberating influence on each other's beliefs, allowing there to be continued growth and evolution together. You encourage each other's radical freedom, for good or ill. If ungrounded, this combination can lead to reckless, speculative behavior with no thought of caution.

Harmonious

This motivates the two of you to look for growth beyond your relationship together. You support each other's independent views and opinions, encouraging each other to constantly expand on your experiences and learn from life. Travel, education, and spiritual growth are all favored.

Challenging

Although this combination promotes a great deal of excitement, you too easily encourage each other into rash and even reckless behavior. There is an unfounded feeling of luck that encourages risk taking that can be disastrous. Arguments can flair up over political and religious issues that you are not likely to see eye to eye on.

Your Jupiter in Aspect to Partner's Neptune

Conjunction

The best of this aspect can lead to providing each other with spiritual insights and bursts of pure inspired creativity. The danger is looking at the world through rose-colored glasses, which can be pleasant enough in the moment, but can also lead to the problems that come from avoidance, denial, and escapism.

Harmonious

Mysticism and philosophical exchanges are favored with this combination, and your discussions help you both rise above the petty issues in life to gain a more inspired view.

Challenging

You encourage each other into blind spots and plans based on false optimism. With this aspect, it is always best to think things all the way through before heading off on a fantasy. You can encourage indulgent behavior in each other, and this could be trouble if either of you has problems with escapism or addictions.

Your Jupiter in Aspect to Partner's Pluto

Conjunction

This aspect awakens powerful ambitions to experience the fullness of life together. This gives you the united strength to achieve shared goals as if you were fulfilling a purpose. This combination can fuel a strong drive to teach and have an impact through religion, education, or politics. You can awaken a hunger in each other to understand the deepest mysteries of life and death.

Harmonious

You can support and take part in mutual interests in travel, education, philosophy, and mysticism. You encourage each other to reach for goals that benefit society as well as yourselves.

Challenging

There is an unconscious pattern of competition between the two of you, and you can goad each other into grander and grander displays of one-upmanship. There can be a natural mistrust of each other's moral and ethical values in how you approach goals.

Your Jupiter in Aspect to Partner's Nodes

Harmonious (*including conjunction to North Node*)

You provide strong support for each other's spiritual growth and can actively pursue spiritual studies together. Travel together can be related to your spiritual quest, and it will not be difficult to find a path that is growth-oriented for both of you.

Challenging (square)

The philosophical and religious interests of the Jupiter person are not growth-oriented for the Nodal person. It would be advisable to encourage and support the differences in your spiritual paths. When you try to find a shared spiritual path, one or the other of you feel as if you are just tagging along.

Conjunction to South Node (opposite North Node)

The past-life karma of this relationship is the Jupiter person having been a teacher or benefactor for the South Node person in a past life. When you first met each other, it was likely a positive experience, and getting to know each other is facilitated by the trust that has already been established.

Your Saturn in Aspect to Partner's Uranus

Conjunction

The best of this aspect is when you help each other to be innovative in how you handle worldly responsibilities. You can assist each other in adapting to changes in the world and evolving your careers to stay in line with your needs for discovery. The low road manifests when the Saturn person resists the innovative ideas of the Uranus person, believing them to be unrealistic and irresponsible, and the Uranus person judges the Saturn person as being stuck in convention and unwilling to experiment in life.

Harmonious

This combination is favorable for working together to fulfill responsibilities of any kind. The Uranus person encourages the Saturn person to be innovative in career considerations, while the Saturn person helps ground the ideas of the Uranus person.

Challenging

There is tension from the Saturn person wanting to maintain the status quo and the Uranus person wanting change. The Saturn person feels the Uranus person is a loose cannon and disruptive to what is going on. The Uranus person becomes frustrated by the Saturn person's narrow thinking.

Your Saturn in Aspect to Partner's Neptune

Conjunction

The best of this combination is when the Saturn person grounds the Neptune person's imagination and helps find ways of manifesting this in the world. It is also favorable when the Neptune person inspires the Saturn person to open to a reality beyond worldly responsibilities. The low road is when the Saturn person doubts and disapproves of the Neptune person's imagination, or when the Neptune person erodes the Saturn person's strength to carry out responsibilities through guilt or fear.

Harmonious

This aspect allows the two of you to handle worldly responsibilities with a sense of grace. The Saturn person helps bring form and structure to the vision of the Neptune person, and the Neptune person inspires the Saturn person to bring vision into his or her career. You can work well together in creative and spiritual pursuits with this combination.

Challenging

You tend to feed each other's doubts and fears, eroding each other's strength. When a cycle of doubt comes over the two of you, it feeds on itself, and soon everything can look bad. This misuse of the imagination needs to be addressed as if it were a test. Discipline needs to be developed to block these negative wanderings of the imagination.

Your Saturn in Aspect to Partner's Pluto

Conjunction

You two have considerable influence and power when you work together. Business and politics would be natural arenas to express the huge power that comes from this combination, and artistic and spiritual types with this aspect would need a huge project to pour this energy into as well. The low road is when the shadow side of power takes over the relationship, leading to blind ambition, corruption, and power conflicts.

Harmonious

You give each other strength and support for tackling large projects, and the two of you together are very effective when dealing with administrative authority. You can count on each other during crunch time, when your back is against the wall.

Challenging

With this aspect, there can be a deep mistrust of each other that will have to be addressed before the relationship can proceed. The Saturn person resents the Pluto person's way of taking control of power. The Pluto person resents the Saturn person's resistance to being directed. Until you work through these issues of mistrust, the threatening feelings you both have may sabotage your attempts to have a healthy relationship.

Your Saturn in Aspect to Partner's Nodes

Conjunction to North Node (opposite South Node)

This can be a very favorable aspect for pursuing a disciplined spiritual path together if, and only if, the North Node person respects the wisdom of the Saturn person. Otherwise, the relationship feels oppressive and growth is blocked.

Conjunction to South Node (opposite North Node)

You carry the past-life karma of the Saturn person having been an authority figure, possibly a parent or teacher, for the South Node person in a past life. The South Node person readily falls into the pattern of deferring to the Saturn person's authority. This will interfere with establishing an equality-based adult relationship, unless the Saturn person compensates for this tendency and refuses to be an authority in any situation the South Node person could handle alone.

Harmonious to Both Nodes

You respect each other's path of soul growth and can help each other stay disciplined on the path. You are able to be patient with each other and help each other get back on track when necessary.

Challenging (square)

You have a difficult time supporting each other's chosen path for soul growth. Until you develop respect for the differences in your paths toward soul growth, you tend to pull each other down more than build each other up.

Your Uranus in Aspect to Partner's Neptune

Harmonious (including conjunction)

There is a creative flow between the Uranus person's intuition and the Neptune person's ability to imagine. This sets up a favorable flow of spiritual guidance that comes to the two of you spontaneously through coincidences and sudden knowing.

Challenging

The Uranus person looks at the Neptune person as being spaced-out. The Neptune person sees the Uranus person as a rebel without a cause. You force each other to examine outdated fads to which you might each be still attached. At a higher level, you force each other to examine the effectiveness of your spiritual techniques and encourage each other to rebel against empty practices that need to be adapted or let go.

Your Uranus in Aspect to Partner's Pluto

Conjunction

You are catalysts for each other to pursue interests beyond the ego. You could fuel each other's interest in social/cultural change, or animate each other's spiritual interests. Your relationship may take on a greater purpose and get pulled into some type of movement together, as in the consciousness movement, the peace movement, or other important social causes.

Harmonious

You support each other's big picture view of what you stand for in life. You can be creative allies in supporting each other's efforts at transforming society through social action, or transforming yourselves through deep spiritual work.

Challenging

Your sense of purpose and life direction may be at odds with each other. The controlling ways of the Pluto person provoke a rebellious independence in the Uranus person, who just seems obstinate to the Pluto person. Can you both accept that your paths might be different, and not try to change each other to your own views?

Your Uranus in Aspect to Partner's Nodes

Conjunction to North Node (opposite South Node)

Soul growth gets put on fast-forward for the two of you. The Uranus person is an evolutionary agent for the North Node person, bringing ideas, experiences, and energy that accelerate the path of awakening. The North Node person helps the Uranus person stay in touch with the prevailing social/cultural climate.

Conjunction to South Node (opposite North Node)

You carry the past-life karma of the Uranus person having been a liberating, but unpredictable, influence in the South Node person's past life. It is as if the two of you had a life-altering fling that awakened parts of you that had been dormant, and then the Uranus person disappeared or moved on. This makes the South Node person feel excited and uneasy simultaneously.

Harmonious to Both Nodes

This aspect is favorable for keeping each other excited about a path of learning from your past and awakening to your future. You come away from discussions feeling excited about the fresh insights you give each other.

Challenging (square)

This aspect presents the challenge of accepting each other's decidedly different views on what constitutes a growth-oriented path. The Nodal person views the Uranus person as being totally unpredictable and unreliable, while the Uranus person thinks it important to shock the Nodal person into awakening to see the big picture.

Your Neptune in Aspect to Partner's Pluto

Conjunction

This aspect can lead to shared interests in large social/cultural reform programs, or the deepest levels of spiritual transformational work. The low road would be getting lost in drugs, alcohol, and escapism as a way of transcending the confines of the everyday world together.

Harmonious

Your interactions with each other invariably help you both rise above the petty, lower currents of reality. If you attempt to meditate together, you will feel as if you are being lifted up on unseen wings.

Challenging

You are prone to promote each other's worst-case fears. You lead each other into the confusion of the shadow world where it is difficult to distinguish between what is real and not real. The test is the right use of your imagination, and the consequences are severe, as is always the case with Pluto challenges. Can you anticipate the absolutely disastrous results that come when you feed each other's fears, and instead train your imaginations not to go down that hellhole of fear? It usually takes meditation training and spiritual practices to get a handle on this subtle, but insidiously powerful, aspect.

Your Neptune in Aspect to Partner's Nodes

Conjunction to North Node (opposite South Node)

This combination is extremely favorable for mutual spiritual and soul growth. When the Neptune person is on track with the highest expression of his or her spirituality, this is perfectly aligned with the North Node person's path for soul growth. Deep interest in mysticism, spirituality, and the transcendent states of consciousness is likely. If neither of you is focusing on your own spiritual growth, this manifests as leading each other down illusionary paths.

Conjunction to South Node (opposite North Node)

The past-life karma that you carry into this life is that of the Neptune person having been a source of spiritual/creative inspiration for the Nodal person in a past life, or having been a master of illusions. To know which is the case for your relationship, ask yourselves if you feel inspired by each other, or if you question if what you share is real. Either way, South Node relationships can seem weird, like something is going on you can't quite put your finger on.

Harmonious to Both Nodes

You can trust each other to provide spiritual guidance and insights as you have a natural empathy for each other's soul needs.

Challenging (square)

You are working through karmic patterns of deception and the tendency to lead each other down paths that ultimately lead to disillusionment. It is important for both of you to compensate for this potential blind spot in your relationship by checking within your own heart of hearts for clarity before following each other's lead.

Your Pluto in Aspect to Partner's Nodes

Conjunction to North Node (opposite South Node)

The soul growth needs of the North Node person bring out the best of the Pluto person's energy. The prospects for taking part in each other's deep spiritual transformation are strong. You can come to greater understandings of the mystery of life by exploring the mystery of death. Practicing yoga, or some other transformational science, would bring out the best of this combination.

Conjunction to South Node (opposite North Node)

Karmic patterns of control games worm their way into the relationship. It is as if the Pluto person can't help but dominate the South Node person, who can't help but submit to the will of the Pluto person. This can bring out destructive behavior patterns in the relationship until the power trips are put behind you. The South Node person is being tested to claim the right to follow his or her personal will, and the Pluto person is being tested with the right use of power. The question is, can this undeniable influence be directed in a way that is in everyone's best interests?

Harmonious to Both Nodes

Your relationship constantly brings you back to the high road of your individual soul paths. You support each other's deep work and draw hidden strength to stay open to transformational work. There is a feeling that you are part of the same soul family, a deeply supportive and strangely familiar tie.

Challenging (square)

A karmic pattern of mistrust must be faced to avoid the undermining influence of this aspect. If issues of mistrust exist, put them on the table and clear the issues before proceeding. Overcome the tendency to let these issues putrefy beneath the surface, which can breed all types of ill feelings.

Your Nodal Axis in Aspect to Partner's Nodes

North and South Nodes Conjunction

Your soul paths are on the same track—where you have been in previous lives and what is growth-oriented for you in this life are the same for both of you. You have natural empathy for each other's history, and a good sense of what is in each other's best interests.

North and South Nodes Opposition

Where you have both been in previous lives and where you are going in this life are exactly opposite. You stand face to face, each of you having been where the other person is going, and because of this you are a valuable resource for each other. But you both are encouraged to remain face to face and not try to change each other to your life direction.

Nodal Axis Harmonious to Both Nodes

Your paths for soul growth in this life naturally support one another. Your histories also lead to a sense of familiarity with each other. You are interested in each other's stories from the past and ideas for future growth.

North and South Nodes Square

Your life paths are at odds with each other. Your personal histories don't promote a natural empathy for what you each have experienced in the past. Making assumptions about each other based on your past experiences always leads to trouble. It is best to treat each other as if you were both raised in separate foreign cultures. This will help you avoid all the troubles that come from taking things for granted about each other that aren't part of the other person's experience at all.

28
Bill and Hillary Clinton's Relationship Astrology

The sheer amount of information that is produced by comparing two charts together can be daunting—the combinations seem endless! How to prioritize your search becomes an issue. First, look for exact conjunctions of one or more planets between the two charts. These conjunctions always become a hot spot in the relationship; something will happen here. When you look at Bill's planet's around Hillary's chart, and her planets around his chart, you immediately see a major conjunction of three of Hillary's planets and four of Bill's planets all in the sign of Leo. Quite the royal couple, these two . . . you know this grouping of planets is going to be a major theater in their relationship. Other exact conjunctions are Hillary's Neptune exactly conjunct Bill's Venus, and Bill's Moon in Taurus conjunct Hillary's North Node. We'll interpret these aspects after we set our game plan.

After exact conjunctions, look for oppositions, which are equally influential in relationships. Oppositions carry the theme of "When they're good, they're very good, and when they're bad they're horrid." Here we see Bill's Moon in Taurus opposite Hillary's Scorpio planets.

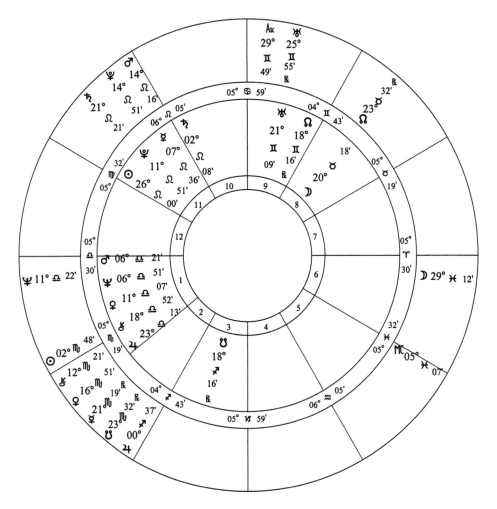

Chart 3
Bill Clinton's Birth Chart,
with Hillary Clinton's Planets in the Outer Wheel

Inner Wheel	**Outer Wheel**
Bill Clinton / August 19, 1946	Hillary Clinton / October 26, 1947
8:51 AM CST / Hope, AR	8:00 PM CST / Chicago, IL
Koch Houses	Koch Houses

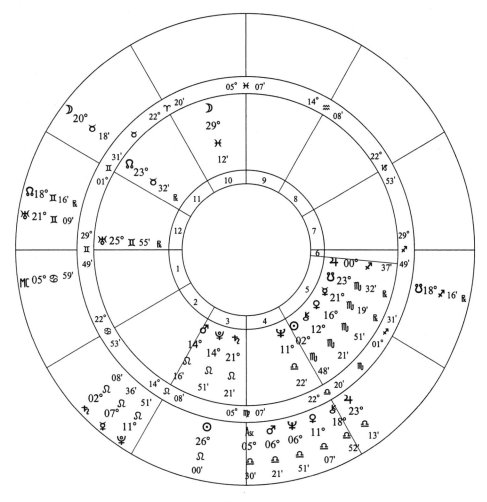

Chart 4
Hillary Clinton's Birth Chart,
with Bill Clinton's Planets in the Outer Wheel

Inner Wheel	**Outer Wheel**
Hillary Clinton / October 26, 1947	Bill Clinton / August 19, 1946
8:00 PM CST / Chicago, IL	8:51 AM CST / Hope, AR
Koch Houses	Koch Houses

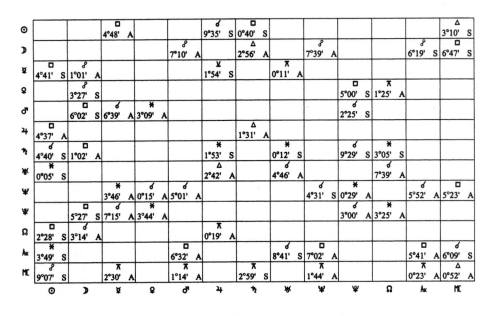

	☉	☽	☿	♀	♂	♃	♄	♅	♆	♇	☊	Asc	MC
☉			□ 4°48' A			☌ 9°35' S	□ 0°40' S						△ 3°10' S
☽					☍ 7°10' A		△ 2°56' A		☍ 7°39' A			☍ 6°19' S	□ 6°47' S
☿	□ 4°41' S	☍ 1°01' A			⚻ 1°54' S		⚻ 0°11' A						
♀		☍ 3°27' S						□ 5°00' S	⚻ 1°25' A				
♂		□ 6°02' S	☌ 6°39' A	⚹ 3°09' A					☌ 2°25' S				
♃	□ 4°37' A						△ 1°31' A						
♄	☌ 4°40' S	□ 1°02' A			⚹ 1°53' S		⚹ 0°12' S		☌ 9°29' S	⚹ 3°05' S			
♅	⚹ 0°05' S				△ 2°42' A		☌ 4°46' A		☌ 7°39' A				
♆		⚹ 3°46' A	☌ 0°15' A	☌ 5°01' A					☌ 4°31' S	⚹ 0°29' A		☌ 5°52' A	□ 5°23' A
♇		□ 5°27' S	☌ 7°15' A	⚹ 3°44' A					☌ 3°00' A	⚹ 3°25' A			
☊	□ 2°28' S	☌ 3°14' A			⚻ 0°19' A								
Asc	⚹ 3°49' S				□ 6°32' A			☌ 8°41' S	□ 7°02' A			□ 5°41' A	☌ 6°09' S
MC	☍ 9°07' S		⚻ 2°30' A		⚻ 1°14' A		⚻ 2°59' S		⚻ 1°44' A			⚻ 0°23' A	△ 0°52' A

Chart 5

Bill and Hillary Clinton's Synastry Table

Next, look for an emphasis of one person's planets falling in a particular house of the other person. These "loaded" houses will always pull the relationship toward issues connected to the dominant houses. Finally, examine the synastry grid for planetary aspects between the two charts, paying particular attention to those aspects that are very close to exact (within two degrees of the exact aspect).

Start by looking for these major themes and then go as deep and detailed as you like. Another good place to start your investigation of two charts is to compare each planet to each other's same planet (Sun to Sun, Moon to Moon, Mercury to Mercury, and so forth).

At first glance of their charts, you wonder how the major grouping of Leo planets in Bill's chart gets along with Hillary's major conjunction of Scorpio planets. Yet, these two appear to be destiny's darlings—they continually rebound from apparent disaster. Somehow their two energies work in ways that don't make sense to the rest of us. Is it a charm, a blessing, or a curse? Their relationship astrology is a bit of an enigma. Leo and Scorpio are not said to get along with one another; they form a square aspect and thus are at odds with one another. They are both fixed signs and often they have difficulty in that neither will back down to the other; they are equally strong and equally resistant to change when pushed. But, as Bill and Hillary have demonstrated, when both are fixed on a common goal, they have tremendous staying power to weather the storms their relationship has endured.

Bill, with the power of Leo and the charm of Libra in his chart, is both benefited and victimized by his own charisma. Hillary's powerful Saturn-Pluto-Mars conjunction sits right on top of Bill's major grouping of Leo planets . . . translation: she's a force he must reckon with. Her Scorpio is on alert and attentive to any infractions of their intimacy, yet she has tolerated and endured the most public exposures to the violation of her trust. And public exposure of private issues is as serious a violation to Scorpio as any other crime, and yet the relationship endures these public inquisitions and goes forward.

Hillary becomes the one voice that Prince Charming must answer to; she's not easily fooled and has the ultimate power of disapproval over his head. But then, he has Saturn exactly square her Sun, so he holds the same power of disapproval over her as she does with him. This leads to détente; the threat of mutual annihilation holds them both in check. A lyric from Bob Dylan's song "Brownsville Girl" comes to mind: "Strange how people who suffer together have stronger connections than people who are most content." Facing challenges together is what they thrive on. Neither can overpower the other, and with mutual acknowledgment of this, all is well. But if there is judgment of their differences, then the fight is on.

Hillary's Mars in Leo (the male energy in her life) is a key to understanding their relationship. Bill is an embodiment of exactly what Hillary wants in a man (Mars). With the authority of Saturn and the power of Pluto in the mix, Bill perfectly acts out what she is to learn from men in her life—the glories, abuses, joys, and battles that come from PMS, "powerful male syndrome." She puts up with the abuses because she doesn't want to let go of the power; or, as one of the political pundits of the era when they lived in the White House said, "She puts up with it because she likes the view from 1600 Pennsylvania Avenue."

In Hillary's chart, Bill's powerful conjunction in Leo squares (challenges) her major grouping of Scorpio planets, including her Venus. Trust/mistrust, abandonment, and betrayal themes are at the core of the vulnerable side of Scorpio. Her South Node in Scorpio also suggests that her past-life karma is loaded with the trust/mistrust scenario. The opposite point, the North Node in Taurus, is her path of soul growth in this life and shows she's hungry for trust and simplicity. She would ultimately benefit from a partner who would say what he means, mean what he says, and then do what he said he would do . . . ah, trust! And Bill's Moon in Taurus is conjunct her North Node, so when he drops into his natural way of being, it soothes her soul. This conjunction falls in her Eleventh House and they keep each other current, informed with the times, and knowing what is going on socially with the big picture. They can also feel comfortable in each other's social circle.

Although Bill's Moon in Taurus feeds Hillary's North Node, it also is exactly opposite her Scorpio planets, particularly her Mercury and Venus. This highly magnetic aspect can lead to misunderstandings and hurt feelings unless great effort is spent to keep the air clear of confusion.

With their Moons in natural harmony with one another (Taurus sextile Pisces), Bill and Hillary's home and personal life together is enhanced. They can enjoy each other's company, and even enjoy downtime together. Their comfort zones are in harmony, which it makes it easier to spend considerable time together. Taurus and Pisces also enjoy each other's tastes in music and the arts, and good food. Sure, they can battle with one another with their Sun signs at odds with each other, but they both can later find refuge in each other's company when its time to pull back and rejuvenate.

Hillary's Gemini Ascendant is in harmony with Bill's Libra Ascendant. These are both air signs, and quite at ease with each other's perspective on life, which is mental for both of them. They value each other's mind, and their ability to engage a friendly rapport allows them to tend to their public image rather gracefully. The air signs' gift, and curse, deals with the ability to detach from the emotional reality of what is going on.

Their Mercurys are part of their Leo/Scorpio square, revealing considerable tension in their communication and many differences of opinion. But here is one of the subtleties of interpretation to pay attention to: The flavor of a planet is altered by the influence of the planets it touches. Bill's Mercury in Leo is conjunct Pluto in his chart, and since Pluto rules Scorpio, his Mercury touching Pluto gives it a Scorpio flavor, giving it an "accidental conjunction" to Hillary's Scorpio Mercury. They are each other's intellectual equal. When they respect each other's differences, bravo, they can sharpen each other's intellect with incisive questions that challenge each other to get to the point. Neither will get the other to back down in an argument . . . again, détente.

Venus and Mars reveal their sexuality and the magnetic spark between the two of them. Bill's Venus is part of a major constellation of planets right near his Ascendant, giving him the gift of charm along with its shadow side, seduction. With Neptune and Mars also part of the mix projecting through his personality, this gives him creativity, drive, and grace, and makes him highly susceptible to delusions. With Hillary's Venus in Scorpio, she sees right through all the pretense and presentation of Bill. He sees someone who sees him for who he truly is, beneath the veneer.

One of the closest aspects in their charts together is the conjunction between Hillary's Neptune and Bill's Venus. On the one hand, we once again see the mutual love of the arts, theater, and music that they can share together. Neptune is a higher octave of Venus (love), and their relationship can take on an archetypal, larger-than-life image for both of them. The higher leanings of this aspect could lead to sacred sexuality and a delightful flair for the imagination in their lovemaking. This all sounds enchanting, and is, but the downside of the same combination can create illusions and even denial of what is really going on in their relationship. If you avoid a small issue and it never comes up again, that is a skill. If you avoid something that needs to be talked about, that is just avoidance.

Examining the synastry grid for the closest aspects between their two charts reveals the strength of their social vision together with Bill's Saturn in trine with Hillary's

Jupiter, and her Jupiter sextile his Jupiter. This creates mutual support and benefit for each other with social and educational choices within their relationship, and also leads to them becoming valuable allies for each other with their political vision. Hillary's Uranus sextiles Bill's Sun, and Bill's Uranus also exactly sextiles Hillary's Saturn, helping them reinvent their lives, again, and again, and again. They support each other's evolutionary awakening and how to look at life through the eye of discovery. Social reforms are at the heart of their relationship.

Of course, the ominous Saturn aspects show up as very close aspects . . . mutual respect, mutual threat. They both hold the hammer of disapproval and judgment over each other's head, but because this is mutual, they can't power-trip each other to get their way—no dominant/submissive games for them. This forces them to negotiate each difference, rather than lock into roles of what happens when push comes to shove. They both know they could annihilate each other, so they don't.

Appendix
Map Your Romantic Relationship
Using the CD-ROM

First you need to install the program. Remove the CD-ROM from its folder and place it in your computer's CD-ROM drive. The program will begin to install itself.

If it does not install automatically, click on the Start menu and select "Run." In the Run menu dialog box, type in your corresponding CD-ROM drive followed by the file name SETUP.exe. Typically, the CD-ROM is set up as D:\. The install wizard will run and guide you through the rest of the process.

For an alternate method, you can access your CD-ROM drive by clicking on "My Computer" and then the CD-ROM drive (typically D:\). Double-click the SETUP.exe icon.

You will see an introductory screen with the name of the program (it flashes on and off very quickly), and then you will see a screen called "Mapping Your Romantic Relationships." This screen is pictured on the following page.

Mapping Your Romantic Relationships is a basic astrology program designed around the most sophisticated astrology programming available. Cosmic Patterns, in collaboration with Llewellyn Worldwide, has developed this program to provide you with birth charts (the circle with all the astrological symbols) and also to provide basic romantic interpretations for two people (ten-page printouts of information about a couple's charts). Let's discuss the choices you have on this screen:

- The Start menu is used to create your charts.
- The About menu provides information about the program; about Llewellyn Worldwide, the publisher of *Mapping Your Romantic Relationships*; and about Cosmic Patterns Software, the designer of the program.
- The Quit menu allows you to exit from the program.

Creating Your Charts and Relationship Interpretation

To use your program, select "Start" from the menu at the top of the screen, and then select "New List of Charts (New Session)." If you are returning to the program and want to see the last chart you made, select "Continue with Charts of Previous Session."

This is where you enter your birth information. There are some simple instructions on the right side of the screen, similar to what follows here. Let's make charts for Bill and Hillary Clinton as an example.

- In the Name box, type "Bill Clinton," and Enter.
- In the Date box, type "08191946" (for August 19, 1946), and Enter.
- In the Time field, type "085100 AM" (the birth time of 8:51 AM in "hh mm ss" format), and Enter.
- In the Place box, type "Hope, Arkansas" (the birth place). As soon as you type the word "Hope," a list drops down. You will notice that Hope, Arkansas, isn't in the list, but Hope is close to Texarkana, Arkansas. So instead, begin typing "Texarkana." When you have typed "Tex," Texarkana, Arkansas, will appear at the top of the list. Select it. The drop-down list disappears, and you will see Texarkana, Arkansas, in the Place box. You will also see information filled in the

boxes below it: the latitude is 33N26 00, the longitude is 094W03 00, the time zone is 6 hours 0 minutes West, and the Daylight Saving Time box is marked "N."

If your city does not automatically come up in the list, you can use a nearby city from the list, just like we did in this example. You can also look up your birth place in an atlas to find the latitude and longitude, time zone, and daylight saving time information. A city close to the birth place is close enough for most purposes and will also be in the same time zone. If the time zone information is different, your chart could be off by an hour one way or the other. Depending on the distance your choice is from your actual birth place, your chart will be slightly different. You can obtain the correct longitude, latitude, and time information from a Time Table book for astrology.[1]

The Zodiac/House button allows you to select a different house system. The program automatically selects the tropical zodiac and Koch house system. Experiment with the other choices to see what changes on the chart wheel.

Select the Save button at the bottom of the screen to save the chart (you can delete it later if you need to), and then click "OK."

Then select the "Done" button. If you forget to save and go directly to the Done button, you will get a prompt asking if you want to save the data. In fact, all the way along, prompts appear to help you enter the data.

You now see an Information box that says "You will now be prompted to enter the data for the second person." Click "OK." Follow the same procedure again by typing "Hillary Clinton," "10261947," and "080000 PM" (Hillary was born on October 26, 1947, at 8:00 PM in Chicago, Illinois). In the Place field, type "Chicago." You will see Chicago Heights and Chicago in the drop-down list. Select "Chicago," "Save," "OK," and "Done."

The screen on the next page is what you will see when you have chosen the "Done" button.

---

1. Here are two possibilities: *The American Atlas,* compiled and programmed by Neil F. Michelsen (San Diego, CA: ACS Publications, 1978); and *The International Atlas,* compiled and programmed by Thomas G. Shanks (San Diego, CA: ACS Publications, 1985).

```
┌──────────────────────────────────────────────────────────────────┐
│ ▓ Mapping Your Romantic Relationship Report            _ ▢ ✕       │
│ File  Reports  Print  Exit                                         │
├──────────────────────────────────────────────────────────────┬───┤
│                                                                │ ▲ │
│                                                                ├───┤
│                                                                │   │
│           Mapping Your Romantic Relationship                   │   │
│                                                                │   │
│                        Report                                  │   │
│                                                                │   │
│                         for                                    │   │
│                                                                │   │
│           Bill Clinton and Hillary Clinton                     │   │
│                                                                │   │
│                         by                                     │   │
│                                                                │   │
│                      David Pond                                │   │
│                                                                │   │
│                                                                │   │
│                                                                │   │
│              Birth Data for Bill Clinton:                      │   │
│                                                                │   │
│                     Bill Clinton                               │   │
│                                                                │   │
│                   August 19, 1946                              │   │
│                                                                ├───┤
│                      8:51 AM                                   │ ▼ │
└────────────────────────────────────────────────────────────────────┘
```

If you scroll down, the names of the charts you just entered appear. You can see Bill and Hillary's names and birth data. If you scroll down, you can see more information lists, and then the interpretation.

If you select "Wheel" from the Reports menu, a form appears. It contains a chart for Bill at the top and one for Hillary at the bottom, and is pictured here.

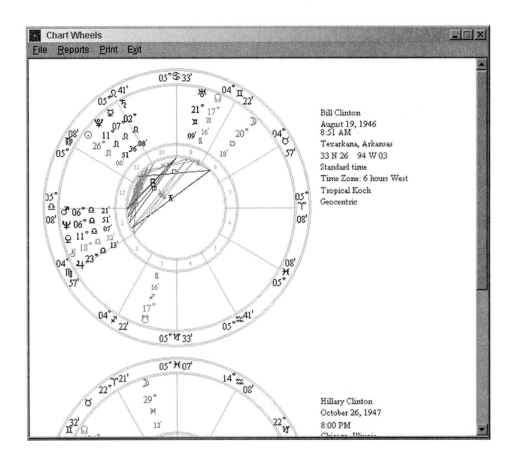

Select "Print" and Print Current Report" to print either the wheel or the interpretation report. Only the item on the screen prints. Select the other option on the Reports menu to change the screen.

Select "Exit" and then "Yes" to go to the opening screen. From here you can either exit the program, or select "Start" to make another chart and interpretation.

That's it! You can now create charts and interpretations for any birth information you want. This program is so easy to use that you won't need much help.

Suggested Reading List

Clement, Stephanie Jean, Ph.D. *Mapping Your Birthchart*. St. Paul, MN: Llewellyn Publications, 2002.

Forrest, Steven. *The Inner Sky*. New York: Bantam Books, 1984.

Greene, Liz. *Relating*. York Beach, ME: Samuel Weiser, 1978.

Hand, Robert. *Horoscope Symbols*. Atglen, PA: Whitford Press, 1981.

Pond, David. *Astrology & Relationships*. St. Paul, MN: Llewellyn Publications, 2001.

Rogers-Gallagher, Kim. *Astrology for the Light Side of the Brain*. San Diego, CA: ACS Publications, 1995.

Wickenburg, Joanne. *A Journey Through the Birth Chart*. Reno, NV: CRCS Publications, 1985.

☾ LLEWELLYN ORDERING INFORMATION

Order Online:
Visit our website at www.llewellyn.com, select your books, and order them on our secure server.

Order by Phone:
- Call toll-free within the U.S. at 1-877-NEW-WRLD (1-877-639-9753). Call toll-free within Canada at 1-866-NEW-WRLD (1-866-639-9753)
- We accept VISA, MasterCard, and American Express

✉ **Order by Mail:**
Send the full price of your order (MN residents add 7% sales tax) in U.S. funds, plus postage & handling to:
Llewellyn Worldwide
P.O. Box 64383, Dept. 0-7387-0420-2
St. Paul, MN 55164-0383, U.S.A.

Postage & Handling:

Standard (U.S., Mexico, & Canada). If your order is:
Up to $25.00, add $3.50
$25.01 - $48.99, add $4.00
$49.00 and over, FREE STANDARD SHIPPING
(Continental U.S. orders ship UPS. AK, HI, PR, & P.O. Boxes ship USPS 1st class. Mex. & Can. ship PMB.)

International Orders:
Surface Mail: For orders of $20.00 or less, add $5 plus $1 per item ordered. For orders of $20.01 and over, add $6 plus $1 per item ordered.

Air Mail:
Books: Postage & Handling is equal to the total retail price of all books in the order.
Non-book items: Add $5 for each item.

Orders are processed within 2 business days. Please allow for normal shipping time.
Postage and handling rates subject to change.

ALL AROUND THE ZODIAC

Exploring Astrology's Twelve Signs

BIL TIERNEY

A fresh, in-depth perspective on the zodiac you thought you knew. This book provides a revealing new look at the astrological signs, from Aries to Pisces. Gain a deeper understanding of how each sign motivates you to grow and evolve in consciousness. How does Aries work with Pisces? What does Gemini share in common with Scorpio? *All Around the Zodiac* is the only book on the market to explore these sign combinations to such a degree.

Not your typical Sun sign guide, this book is broken into three parts. Part 1 defines the signs, part 2 analyzes the expression of sixty-six pairs of signs, and part 3 designates the expression of the planets and houses in the signs.

0-7387-0111-4, 528 pp., 6 x 9   **$17.95**

THE ART OF PREDICTIVE ASTROLOGY
Forecasting Your Life Events

CAROL RUSHMAN

Become an expert at seeing the future in anyone's astrological chart! Insight into the future is a large part of the intrigue and mystery of astrology. *The Art of Predictive Astrology* clearly lays out a step-by-step system that astrologers can use to forecast significant events including love and financial success. When finished with the book, readers will be able to predict cycles and trends for the next several years, and give their clients fifteen important dates for the coming year. An emphasis is on progressions, eclipses, and lunations as important predictive tools.

0-7387-0164-5, 288 pp., 6 x 9 $14.95

ASTROLOGY
Understanding the Birth Chart

KEVIN BURK

This beginning-to intermediate-level astrology book is based on a course taught to prepare students for the NCGR Level I Astrological Certification exam. It is a unique book for several reasons. First, rather than being an astrological phrase book or "cookbook," it helps students to understand the language of astrology. From the beginning, students are encouraged to focus on the concepts, not the keywords. Second, as soon as you are familiar with the fundamental elements of astrology, the focus shifts to learning how to work with these basics to form a coherent, synthesized interpretation of a birth chart.

In addition, it explains how to work with traditional astrological techniques, most notably the essential dignities. All interpretive factors are brought together in the context of a full interpretation of the charts of Sylvester Stallone, Meryl Streep, Eva Peron, and Woody Allen. This book fits the niche between cookbook astrology books and more technical manuals.

1-56718-088-4, 384 pp., 7½ x 9⅛, illus.   **$17.95**

ASTROLOGY & RELATIONSHIPS
Techniques for Harmonious Personal Connections

DAVID POND

Take your relationships to a deeper level. There is a hunger for intimacy in the modern world. *Astrology & Relationships* is a guidebook on how to use astrology to improve all your relationships. This is not fortunetelling astrology, predicting which signs you will be most compatible with; instead, it uses astrology as a model to help you experience greater fulfillment and joy in relating to others. You can also look up your planets, and those of others, to discover specific relationship needs and talents.

What makes this book unique is that it goes beyond descriptive astrology to suggest methods and techniques for actualizing the stages of a relationship that each planet represents. Many of the exercises are designed to awaken individual skills and heighten self-understanding, leading you to first identify a particular quality within yourself, and then to relate to it in others.

0-7387-0046-0, 368 pp., 7½ x 9⅛   **$17.95**